Collins

2019 GUIDE
to the
NIGHT SKY

SOUTHERN HEMISPHERE

Storm Dunlop and Wil Tirion

Published by Collins
An imprint of HarperCollins Publishers
Westerhill Road
Bishopbriggs
Glasgow G64 2QT
www.harpercollins.co.uk

© HarperCollins Publishers 2018
Text and illustrations © Storm Dunlop and Wil Tirion
Photographs © see acknowledgements page 94.

Collins ® is a registered trademark of HarperCollins Publishers Ltd

The contents of this publication are believed correct at the time of printing.
Nevertheless the publisher can accept no responsibility for errors or omissions,
changes in the detail given or for any expense or loss thereby caused.

HarperCollins does not warrant that any website mentioned in this title will be provided uninterrupted,
that any website will be error free, that defects will be corrected, or that the website or the server that
makes it available are free of viruses or bugs. For full terms and conditions please refer to the site
terms provided on the website.

A catalogue record for this book is available from the British Library

ISBN 978-0-00-829499-1

10 9 8 7 6 5 4 3 2 1

Printed in China by RR Donnelley APS

If you would like to comment on any aspect of this book, please contact us at the above address or online.
e-mail: collinsmaps@harpercollins.co.uk

 facebook.com/CollinsAstronomy

 @CollinsAstro

MIX
Paper from
responsible sources

FSC
www.fsc.org   **FSC™ C007454**

This book is produced from independently certified
FSC™ paper to ensure responsible forest management.

For more information visit: www.harpercollins.co.uk/green

Contents

Introduction

The aim of this Guide is to help people find their way around the night sky, by showing how the stars that are visible change from month to month and by including details of various events that occur throughout the year. The objects and events described may be observed with the naked eye, or nothing more complicated than a pair of binoculars.

The conditions for observing naturally vary over the course of the year. During the summer, twilight may persist throughout the night and make it difficult to see the faintest stars. There are three recognized stages of twilight: civil twilight, when the Sun is less than 6° below the horizon; nautical twilight, when the Sun is between 6° and 12° below the horizon; and astronomical twilight, when the Sun is between 12° and 18° below the horizon. Full darkness occurs only when the Sun is more than 18° below the horizon. During nautical twilight, only the very brightest (navigation) stars are visible. During astronomical twilight, the faintest stars visible to the naked eye may be seen directly overhead, but are lost at lower altitudes. At Sydney, full darkness persists for about six hours at mid-summer. Even at Christchurch, NZ (not shown), full darkness

lasts about four hours. By contrast, as far south as Cape Horn, at mid-summer nautical twilight persists, so only the very brightest stars are visible.

Another factor that affects the visibility of objects is the amount of moonlight in the sky. At Full Moon, it may be very difficult to see some of the fainter stars and objects, and even when the Moon is at a smaller phase it may seriously interfere with visibility if it is near the stars or planets in which you are interested. A full lunar calendar is given for each month and may be used to see when nights are likely to be darkest and best for observation.

The celestial sphere

All the objects in the sky (including the Sun, Moon and stars) appear to lie at some indeterminate distance on a large sphere, centred on the Earth. This *celestial sphere* has various reference points and features that are related to those of the Earth. If the Earth's rotational axis is extended, for example, it points to the North and South Celestial Poles, which are thus in line with the North and South Poles on Earth. Similarly, the *celestial equator* lies in the same plane as the Earth's equator,

The duration of twilight throughout the year at Sydney and Cape Horn.

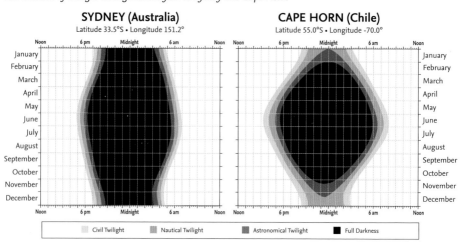

and divides the sky into northern and southern hemispheres. Because this Guide is written for use in the southern hemisphere, the area of the sky that it describes includes the whole of the southern celestial hemisphere and those portions of the northern that become visible at different times of the year. Stars in the far north, however, remain invisible throughout the year, and are not included.

It is useful to know some of the special terms for various parts of the sky. As seen by an observer, half of the celestial sphere is invisible, below the horizon. The point directly overhead is known as the **zenith**, and the (invisible) one below one's feet as the **nadir**. The line running from the north point on the horizon, up through the zenith and then down to the south point is the **meridian**. This is an important invisible line in the sky, because objects are highest in the sky, and thus easiest to see, when they cross the meridian in the south. Objects are said to **transit**, when they cross this line in the sky.

In this book, reference is frequently made in the text and in the diagrams to the standard compass points around the horizon. The position of any object in the sky may be described by its **altitude** (measured in degrees

above the horizon), and its **azimuth** (measured in degrees from north 0°, through east 90°, south 180° and west 270°). Experienced amateurs and professional astronomers also use another system of specifying locations on the celestial sphere, but that need not concern us here, where the simpler method will suffice.

The celestial sphere appears to rotate about an invisible axis, running between the North and South Celestial Poles. The location (i.e., the altitude) of the Celestial Poles depends entirely on the observer's position on Earth or, more specifically, their latitude. The charts in this book are produced for the latitude of 35°S, so the South Celestial Pole (SCP) is 35° above the southern horizon. The fact that the SCP is fixed relative to the horizon means that all the stars within 35° of the pole are always above the horizon and may, therefore, always be seen at night, regardless of the time of year. The southern circumpolar region is an ideal place to begin learning the sky, and ways to identify the circumpolar stars and constellations will be described shortly.

The ecliptic and the zodiac
Another important line on the celestial sphere is the Sun's apparent path against

Measuring altitude and azimuth on the celestial sphere.

The altitude of the South Celestial Pole equals the observer's latitude.

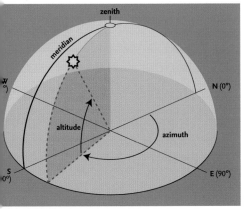

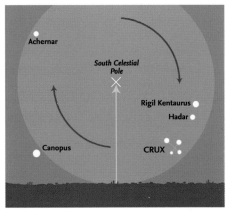

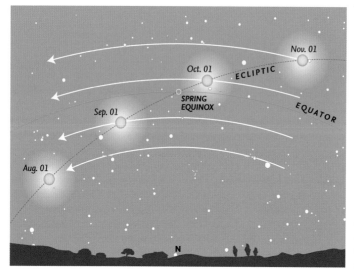

The Sun crossing the celestial equator at the September equinox (spring equinox in the southern hemisphere).

the background stars – in reality the result of the Earth's orbit around the Sun. This is known as the *ecliptic*. The point where the Sun, apparently moving along the ecliptic, crosses the celestial equator from south to north is known as the (southern) autumn equinox, which occurs on March 20 or 21. At this time and at the (southern) spring equinox, on September 22 or 23, when the Sun crosses the celestial equator from north to south, day and night are almost exactly equal in length. (There is a slight difference, but that need not concern us here.) The March equinox is currently located in the constellation of Pisces, and is important in astronomy because it defines the zero point for a system of celestial coordinates, which is, however, not used in this Guide.

The Moon and planets are to be found in a band of sky that extends 8° on either side of the ecliptic. This is because the orbits of the Moon and planets are inclined at various angles to the ecliptic (i.e., to the plane of the Earth's orbit). This band of sky is known as the zodiac and, when originally devised, consisted of twelve *constellations*, all of which were considered to be exactly 30° wide. When the constellation boundaries were formally established by the International Astronomical Union in 1930, the exact extent of most constellations was altered and, nowadays, the ecliptic passes through thirteen constellations. Because of the boundary changes, the Moon and planets may actually pass through several other constellations that are adjacent to the original twelve.

The constellations

Since ancient times, the celestial sphere has been divided into various constellations, most dating back to antiquity and usually associated with certain myths or legendary people and animals. Nowadays, the boundaries of the constellations have been fixed by international agreement and their names (in Latin) are largely derived from Greek or Roman originals. Some of the names of the most prominent stars are of Greek or Roman origin, but many are derived from Arabic names. Many bright stars have no individual names and, for many years, stars were identified by terms such as 'the star in Hercules' right foot'. A more sensible scheme was introduced by the German astronomer Johannes Bayer in the early seventeenth century. Following his scheme – which is still used today – most of the brightest stars are identified by a Greek letter followed by the genitive form of the constellation's Latin name. An example is the Pole Star, also known as Polaris and α Ursae Minoris (abbreviated α UMi). The Greek alphabet is shown on page 94 and a list of all the constellations that may be seen from latitude 35°S, together with abbreviations, their genitive forms and English names is on page 93. Other naming schemes exist for fainter stars, but are not used in this book.

Asterisms

Apart from the constellations (88 of which cover the whole sky), certain groups of stars, which may form a part of a larger constellation or cross several constellations, are readily recognizable and have been given individual names. These groups are known as **asterisms**, and the most famous (and well-known to northern observers) is the 'Plough', the common name for the seven brightest stars in the constellation of Ursa Major, the Great Bear. The names and details of some asterisms mentioned in this book are given in the list on page 94.

Magnitudes

The brightness of a star, planet or other body is frequently given in magnitudes (mag.). This is a mathematically defined scale where larger numbers indicate a fainter object. The scale extends beyond the zero point to negative numbers for very bright objects. (Sirius, the brightest star in the sky is mag. -1.4.) Most observers are able to see stars to about mag. 6, under very clear skies.

The Moon

Although the daily rotation of the Earth carries the sky from east to west, the Moon gradually moves eastwards by approximately its diameter (about half a degree) in an hour. Normally, in its orbit around the Earth, the Moon passes above or below the direct line between Earth and Sun (at New Moon) or outside the area obscured by the Earth's shadow (at Full Moon). Occasionally, however, the three bodies are more-or-less perfectly aligned to give an **eclipse**: a solar eclipse at New Moon or a lunar eclipse at Full Moon. Depending on the exact circumstances, a solar eclipse may be merely partial (when the Moon does not cover the whole of the Sun's disk); annular (when the Moon is too far from Earth in its orbit to appear large enough to hide the whole of the Sun); or total. Total and annular eclipses are visible from very restricted areas of the Earth, but partial eclipses are normally visible over a wider area.

Somewhat similarly, at a lunar eclipse, the Moon may pass through the outer zone of the Earth's shadow, the **penumbra** (in a penumbral eclipse, which is not generally perceptible to the naked eye), so that just part of the Moon is within the darkest part of the Earth's shadow, the **umbra** (in a partial eclipse); or completely within the umbra (in a total eclipse). Unlike solar eclipses, lunar eclipses are visible from large areas of the Earth.

Occasionally, as it moves across the sky, the Moon passes between the Earth and individual planets or distant stars, giving rise to an **occultation**. As with solar eclipses, such occultations are visible from restricted areas of the world.

The planets

Because the planets are always moving against the background stars, they are treated in some detail in the monthly pages and information is given when they are close to other planets, the Moon or any of five bright stars that lie near the ecliptic. Such events are known as **appulses** or, more frequently, as **conjunctions**. (There are technical differences in the way these terms are defined – and should be used – in astronomy, but these need not concern us here.) The positions of the planets are shown for every month on a special chart of the ecliptic.

The term conjunction is also used when a planet is either directly behind or in front of the Sun, as seen from Earth. (Under normal circumstances it will then be invisible.) The conditions of most favourable visibility depend on whether the planet is one of the two known

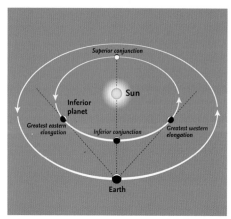

Inferior planet.

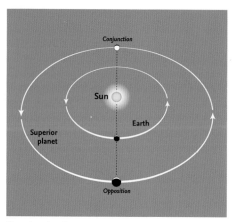

Superior planet.

as **inferior planets** (Mercury and Venus) or one of the three **superior planets** (Mars, Jupiter and Saturn) that are covered in detail. (Some details of the fainter superior planets, Uranus and Neptune, are included in this Guide, and special charts for both are given on pages 77 and 71.)

The inferior planets are most readily seen at eastern or western **elongation**, when their angular distance from the Sun is greatest. For superior planets, they are best seen at **opposition**, when they are directly opposite the Sun in the sky, and cross the meridian at local midnight.

It is often useful to be able to estimate angles on the sky, and approximate values may be obtained by holding one hand at arm's length. The various angles are shown in the diagram, together with the separations of the various stars in and around Orion.

Meteors

At some time or other, nearly everyone has seen a **meteor** – a 'shooting star' – as it flashed across the sky. The particles that cause meteors – known technically as 'meteoroids' – range in size from that of a grain of sand (or even smaller) to the size of a pea. On any night of the year there are occasional meteors, known as **sporadics**, that may travel in any direction. These occur at a rate that is normally between three and eight in an hour. Far more important, however, are **meteor showers**, which occur at fixed periods of the year, when the Earth encounters a trail of particles left behind by a comet or, very occasionally, by a minor planet (asteroid). Meteors always appear to diverge from a single point on the sky, known as the **radiant**, and the radiants of major showers are shown on the charts. Meteors that come from a circular area 8° in diameter around the radiant are classed as belonging to the particular shower. All others that do not come from that area are sporadics (or, occasionally from another shower that is active at the same time). A list of the major meteor showers is given on page 17.

Although the positions of the various shower radiants are shown on the charts, looking directly at the radiant is not the most effective way of seeing meteors. They are most likely to be noticed if one is looking about 40–45° away from the radiant position. (This is approximately two hand-spans as shown in the diagram for measuring angles.)

Other objects

Certain other objects may be seen with the naked eye under good conditions. Some were given names in antiquity – Praesepe is one example – but many are known by what are called 'Messier numbers', the numbers in a catalogue of nebulous objects compiled by Charles Messier in the late eighteenth century.

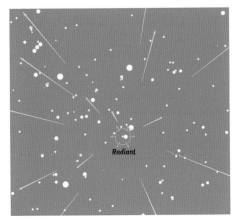

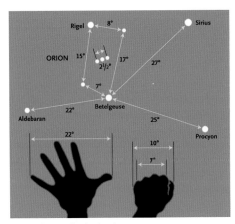

Meteor shower (showing the Geminids radiant).

Measuring angles in the sky.

Some, such as the Andromeda Galaxy, M31, and the Orion Nebula, M42, may be seen by the naked eye, but all those given in the list will benefit from the use of binoculars. Apart from galaxies, such as M31, which contain thousands of millions of stars, there are also two types of cluster: open clusters, such as M45, the Pleiades, which may consist of a few dozen to some hundreds of stars; and globular clusters, such as Omega Centauri, which are spherical concentrations of many thousands of stars. One or two gaseous nebulae (emission nebulae), consisting of gas illuminated by stars within them, are also visible. The Orion Nebula, M42, is one, and is illuminated by the group of four stars, known as the Trapezium, which may be seen within it by using a good pair of binoculars.

Some interesting objects.

Messier / NGC	Name	Type	Constellation	Maps (months)
—	47 Tucanae	globular cluster	Tucana	All year
—	Hyades	open cluster	Taurus	Sep. – Apr.
—	Melotte 111 (Coma Cluster)	open cluster	Coma Berenices	Jan. – Aug.
M3	—	globular cluster	Canes Venatici	Jan. – Sep.
M4	—	globular cluster	Scorpius	May – Aug.
M8	Lagoon Nebula	gaseous nebula	Sagittarius	Jun. – Sep.
M11	Wild Duck Cluster	open cluster	Scutum	May – Oct.
M13	Hercules Cluster	globular cluster	Hercules	Feb. – Nov.
M15	—	globular cluster	Pegasus	Jun. – Dec.
M22	—	globular cluster	Sagittarius	Jun. – Sep.
M27	Dumbbell Nebula	planetary nebula	Vulpecula	May – Dec.
M31	Andromeda Galaxy	galaxy	Andromeda	All year
M35	—	open cluster	Gemini	Oct. – May
M42	Orion Nebula	gaseous nebula	Orion	Nov. – Mar.
M44	Praesepe	open cluster	Cancer	Nov. – Jun.
M45	Pleiades	open cluster	Taurus	Aug. – Apr.
M57	Ring Nebula	planetary nebula	Lyra	Apr. – Dec.
M67	—	open cluster	Cancer	Dec. – May
IC 2602	Southern Pleiades	open cluster	Carina	Nov. – Aug.
NGC 2070	Tarantula Nebula	emission nebula	Dorado (LMC)	All year
NGC 3242	Ghost of Jupiter	planetary nebula	Hydra	Feb. – May
NGC 3372	Eta Carinae Nebula	gaseous nebula	Carina	Nov. – Aug.
NGC 4755	Jewel Box	open cluster	Crux	Dec. – Aug.
NGC 5139	Omega Centauri	globular cluster	Centaurus	Jan. – Aug.

The Southern Circumpolar Constellations

The southern circumpolar constellations are the key to to starting to identify the constellations. For anyone in the southern hemisphere they are visible at any time of the year, and nearly everyone is familiar with the striking pattern of four stars that make up the constelllation of **Crux** (the Southern Cross), and also the two nearby bright stars **Rigil Kentaurus** and **Hadar** (α and β Centauri respectively). This pattern of stars is visible throughout the year for most observers, although for observers farther north, the stars may become difficult to see, low on the horizon in the southern spring, espcially in the months of October and November.

Crux

The distinctive shape of the constellation of **Crux** is usually easy to identify although some people (especially northerners unused to the southern sky) may wrongly identify the slightly larger False Cross, formed by the stars **Aspidiske** and **Avior** (ι and ε Carinae respectively) plus κ and δ Velorum. The dark patch of the Coalsack (a dark cloud of obscuring dust) is readily visible on the eastern side between **Acrux** and **Mimosa** (α and β Crucis).

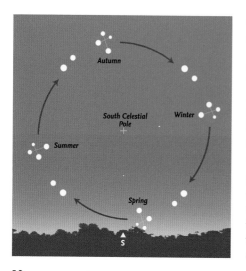

A line through **Gacrux** (γ Crucis) and **Acrux** (α Crucis) points approximately in the direction of the South Celestial Pole, crossing the faint constellations of **Musca** and **Chamaeleon**. Although there is no bright star close to the South Celestial Pole (and even the constellation in which it lies, Octans, is faint), an idea of its location helps to identify the region of sky that is always visible. (The altitude of the South Celestial Pole is equal to the observer's latitude south of the equator.) The basic triangular shape of Octans itself is best found by extending a line from **Peacock** (α Pavonis) through β Pavonis, by about the same distance as that between the stars.

Centaurus

Although Crux is a distinctive shape, **Centaurus** is a large, rather straggling constellation, with one notable object, the giant, bright globular cluster **Omega Centauri** (the brightest globular in the sky), which lies towards the north, on the line from **Hadar** (β Centauri), through ε Centauri. Rather than locating the South Celestial Pole from Crux, a better indication is the line, at right angles to the line between Hadar and Rigil Kentaurus that passes along the brightest star in **Circinus** (α).

Carina

Apart from the two stars that form part of the False Cross, the constellation of Carina is, like Centaurus, a large, sprawling constellation. It contains one striking open cluster, the **Southern Pleiades**, and a remarkable emission nebula, the **Eta Carinae Nebula**. The second brightest star in the sky (after Sirius) is **Canopus**, α Carinae, which lies far away to the west.

The Magellanic Clouds

On the opposite side of the South Celestial Pole to Crux and Centaurus lie the two Magellanic Clouds. The **Small Magellanic Cloud** (SMC) lies to one side of the relatively inconspicuous, triangular constellation of **Hydrus**, but is actually within the constellation of **Tucana**.

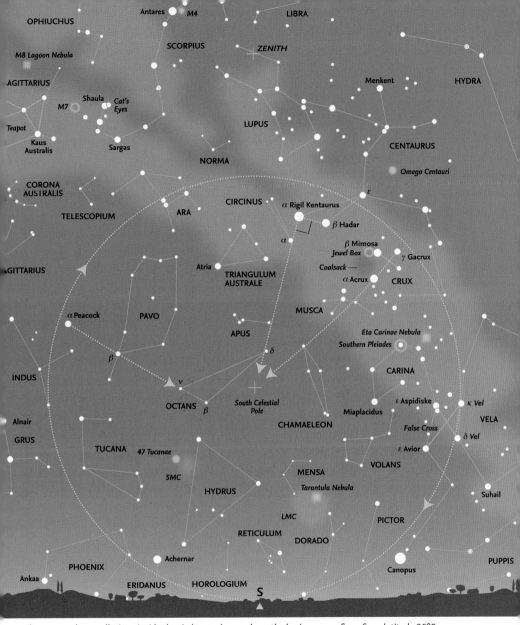

The stars and constellations inside the circle are always above the horizon, seen from from latitude 35°S.

Nearby is another bright globular cluster, **47 Tucanae.** Hydrus itself is also easily identified from the star, **Achernar**, α Eridani, the rather isolated brilliant star at the southern end of **Eridanus**, which wanders a long way south, having begun at the foot of Orion.

The **Large Magellanic Cloud** (LMC) lies within the faint constellation of **Dorado**. Not only is it a large satellite galaxy of the Milky Way Galaxy, but it contains the large, readily visible, **Tarantula Nebula**, an emission nebula that is a major star-forming region.

Comet C/2006 P1 McNaught, imaged on 20 January 2007, from Lawlers Gold Mine, Western Australia (Photographer: Sjbmgrtl).

The Murchison meteorite

The year 2019 includes the 50th anniversary of the arrival of the Murchison meteorite, which fell near Murchison, Victoria, Australia, on 28 September 1969. The total mass of fragments collected is over 100 kg: and the one illustrated is now in the National Museum of Natural History, in Washington, D.C. The meteorite proved to be a carbonaceous chondrite, and as such, is one of the most primitive types of meteorites, representative of the primordial material from which the Solar System was formed. The meteorite has been extensively studied and is particularly rich in organic compounds, such as amino acids (the building blocks of life). Many thousands of chemical compounds have been identified in this object, more than in any other meteorite.

Comets and the Moon

Comets

Although comets may occasionally become very striking objects in the sky, their occurrence and particularly the existence or length of any tail and their overall magnitude are notoriously difficult to predict. Naturally, it is only possible to predict the return of periodic comets (whose names have the prefix 'P'). Many comets appear unexpectedly (these have names with the prefix 'C'). Bright, readily visible comets such as C/1995 Y1 Hyakutake & C/1995 O1 Hale-Bopp or C/2006 P1 McNaught (sometime known as the Great Comet of 2007) are rare. (Comet Hale-Bopp, in particular, was visible for a record 18 months and was a prominent object in northern skies.) Comet McNaught was notable for its multiple tail structure. Most periodic comets are faint and only a very small number ever become bright enough to be readily visible with the naked eye or with binoculars. No bright comets are predicted to be visible from the southern hemisphere in 2019.

Comet C/2014 Q2 Lovejoy, which reached naked-eye visibility, photographed on 20 December 2014, when in Columba, by Damian Peach.

The Moon

The monthly pages include diagrams showing the phase of the Moon for every day of the month, and also indicate the day in the **lunation** (or *age* of the Moon), which begins at New Moon. Although the main features of the surface – the light highlands and the dark maria (seas) – may be seen with the naked eye, far more features may be detected with the use of binoculars or any telescope. The many craters are best seen when they are close to the **terminator** (the boundary between the illuminated and the non-illuminated areas of the surface), when the Sun rises or sets over any particular region of the Moon and the crater walls or central peaks cast strong shadows. Most features become difficult to see at Full Moon, although this is the best time to see the bright ray systems surrounding certain craters. Accompanying the Moon map on the following pages is a list of prominent features, including the days in the lunation when features are normally close to the terminator and thus easiest to see. A few bright features such as Linné and Proclus, visible when well illuminated, are also listed. One feature, Rupes Recta (the Straight Wall) is readily visible only when it casts a shadow with light from the east, appearing as a light line when illuminated from the opposite direction.

The dates of visibility vary slightly through the effects of **libration**. Because the Moon's orbit is inclined to the Earth's equator and also because it moves in an ellipse, the Moon appears to rock slightly from side to side (and nod up and down). Features near the **limb** (the edge of the Moon) may vary considerably in their location and visibility. (This is easily noticeable with Mare Crisium and the craters Tycho and Plato.) Another effect is that at crescent phases before and after New Moon, the normally non-illuminated portion of the Moon receives a certain amount of light, reflected from the Earth. This **Earthshine** may enable certain bright features (such as Aristarchus, Kepler and Copernicus) to be detected even though they are not illuminated by sunlight.

Map of the Moon

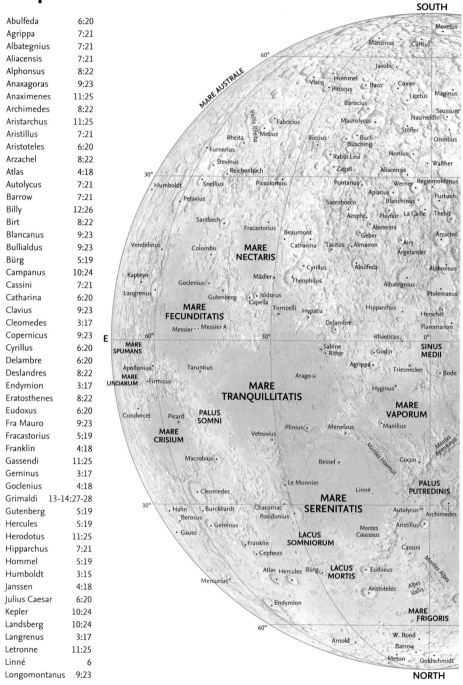

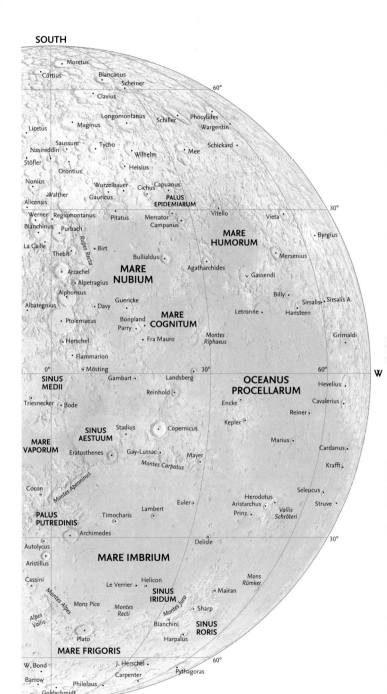

SOUTH

NORTH

W

MAP OF THE MOON **15**

Introduction to the Month-by-Month Guide

The monthly charts

The pages devoted to each month contain a pair of charts showing the appearance of the night sky, looking south and looking north. The charts (as with all the charts in this book) are drawn for the latitude of 35°S, so observers farther north will see slightly more of the sky on the northern horizon, and slightly less on the southern, with corresponding changes if they are farther south. The horizon areas are, of course, those most likely to be affected by poor observing conditions caused by haze, mist or smoke. In addition, stars close to the horizon are always dimmed by atmospheric absorption, so sometimes the faintest stars marked on the charts may not be visible.

The three times shown for each chart require a little explanation. The charts are drawn to show the appearance at 11 p.m. for the 1st of each month. The same appearance will apply an hour earlier (10 p.m.) on the 15th, and yet another hour earlier (9 p.m.) at the end of the month (shown as the 1st of the following month). Daylight Saving Time (DST) is not used in South Africa. In New Zealand, it applies from the last Sunday of September to the first Sunday of April. In those Australian states with DST, it runs from the first Sunday in October to the first Sunday in April. The appropriate times are shown on the monthly charts. Times of specific events are shown on the 24-hour clock of Universal Time (UT), used by astronomers worldwide, and corrections for the local time zone (and DST where employed) may be found from the details inside the front cover.

The charts may be used for earlier or later times during the night. To observe two hours earlier, use the charts for the preceding month; for two hours later, the charts for the next month.

Meteors

Details of specific meteor showers are given in the months when they come to maximum,

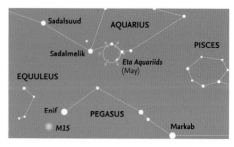

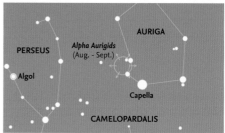

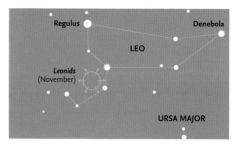

regardless of whether they begin or end in other months. Note that not all the respective radiants are marked on the charts for that particular month, because the radiants may be below the horizon, or lie in constellations that are not readily visible during the month of maximum. For this reason, special charts for the Eta Aquariids (May), the Alpha Aurigids (August & September) and the Leonids (November) are given here. As just explained, however, meteors from such showers may still be seen, because the most effective region for seeing meteors is some 40–45° away from the radiant, and that area of sky may well be above the horizon. A table of the best meteor showers visible during the year is also given here.

Shower	Dates of activity 2019	Date of maximum 2019	Possible hourly rate
Centaurids	January 28 to February 21	February 8	5
Gamma Normids	February 25 to March 22	March 13	6
Pi Puppids	April 15 to April 28	April 23	var.
Eta Aquariids	April 19 to May 26	May 6–7	55
Alpha Capricornids	July 11 to August 10	July 26–August 1	5
Perseids	July 13 to August 26	August 11–12	100
Piscis Austrinids	July 15 to August 10	July 27–28	5
Delta Aquariids	July 21 to August 23	July 29–30	< 20
Alpha Aurigids	August to October	August 28 & September 15	10
Southern Taurids	September 23 to November 19	October 28–29	< 5
Orionids	September 23 to November 27	October 21–22	25
Northern Taurids	October 19 to November 10	November 10–11	< 5
Leonids	November 5 to November 30	November 17–18	< 15
Phoenicids	November 28 to December 9	December 2	var.
Puppid Velids	December 1 to December 15	December 7	10
Geminids	December 4 to December 16	December 13–14	100+

Meteors that are brighter than magnitude -4 (approximately the maximum magnitude reached by Venus) are known as *fireballs* or *bolides*.

The photographs

As an aid to identification – especially as some people find it difficult to relate charts to the actual stars they see in the sky – one or more photographs of constellations visible in certain specific months are included. It should be noted, however, that because of the limitations of the photographic and printing processes, and the differences between the sensitivity of different individuals to faint starlight (especially in their ability to detect different colours), and the degree to which they have become adapted to the dark, the apparent brightness of stars in the photographs will not necessarily precisely match that seen by any one observer.

The Moon calendar

The Moon calendar is largely self-explanatory. It shows the phase of the Moon for every day of the month, with the exact times (in Universal Time) of New Moon, First Quarter, Full Moon, and Last Quarter. Because the times are calculated from the Moon's actual orbital parameters, some of the times shown will, naturally, fall during daylight, but any difference is too small to affect the appearance of the Moon on that date. Also shown is the *age* of the Moon (the day in the *lunation*), beginning at New Moon, which may be used to determine the best time for observation of specific lunar features.

The Moon

The section on the Moon includes details of any lunar or solar eclipses that may occur during the month (visible from anywhere on Earth). Similar information is given about any important occultations. Mainly, however, this section summarizes when the Moon passes close to planets or the five prominent stars close to the ecliptic. The dates when the Moon is closest to the Earth (at *perigee*) and farthest from it (at *apogee*) are shown in the monthly calendars, and only mentioned here when they are particularly significant, such as the nearest and farthest during the year

The planets and minor planets

Brief details are given of the location, movement and brightness of the planets from Mercury to Saturn throughout the month. None of the planets can, of course, be seen when they are close to the Sun, so such periods are generally noted. All of the planets may sometimes lie on the opposite side of the Sun to the Earth (at superior conjunction), but in the case of the inferior planets, Mercury and Venus, they may also pass between the Earth and the Sun (at inferior conjunction)

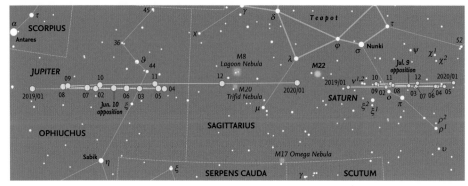

The paths of Jupiter and Saturn in 2019. Jupiter comes to opposition on June 10; Saturn almost a month later, on July 9. Background stars are shown down to magnitude 6.5 (south is up).

and are normally invisible for a longer or shorter period of time. Those two planets are normally easiest to see around either eastern or western elongation, in the evening or morning sky, respectively. Not every elongation is favourable, so although every elongation is listed, only those where observing conditions are favourable are shown in the individual diagrams of events.

The dates at which the superior planets reverse their motion (from direct motion to retrograde, and retrograde to direct) and of opposition (when a planet generally reaches its maximum brightness) are given. Some planets, especially distant Saturn, may spend most or all of the year in a single constellation. Jupiter and Saturn are normally easiest to see around opposition, which occurs every year. Mars, by contrast, moves relatively rapidly against the background stars and in some years never comes to opposition. In 2019, Jupiter and Saturn are close together in the sky throughout the year, so a special chart is shown here.

Uranus is not always included in the monthly details because it is generally at the limit of naked-eye visibility (magnitude 5.7–5.9), although bright enough to be visible in binoculars, or even with the naked eye under exceptionally dark skies. Its path in 2019 is shown on the special chart in October. It comes to opposition on October 28 in the

constellation of Aries. New Moon occurs that day, so the planet, at magnitude 5.7 should be detectable reasonably easily. It is at the same magnitude for an extended period of the year (from August to December) and should be visible when free from interference by moonlight.

Similar considerations apply to Neptune, although this is always fainter (magnitude 7.8–8.0 in 2019), but still visible in most binoculars. It reaches opposition at mag. 7.8 on September 10 in Aquarius. Full Moon occurs four days later, so Neptune will be difficult to detect, for about a week after Full Moon. Again, Neptune's path in 2019 and its position at opposition are shown in a chart in September.

Charts for the three brightest minor planets that come to opposition in 2019 are shown in the relevant month: Pallas (mag. 7.9) on April 10, Ceres (mag. 7.0) on May 28, and Vesta (mag. 6.5) on November 12.

The ecliptic charts

Although the ecliptic charts are primarily designed to show the positions and motions of the major planets, they also show the motion of the Sun during the month. The light-tinted area shows the area of the sky that is invisible during daylight, but the darker area gives an indication of which constellations are likely to be visible at some time of the night. The closer a planet is to the border between dark and light, the more difficult it will be to see in the twilight.

The monthly calendar

For each month, a calendar shows details of significant events, including when planets are close to one another in the sky, close to the Moon, or close to any one of five bright stars that are spaced along the ecliptic. The times shown are given in Universal Time (UT), always used by astronomers throughout the year, and which is identical to Greenwich Mean Time (GMT). So during the summer months, they do not show Summer Time, which will always be one hour later than the time shown.

The diagrams of interesting events

Each month, a number of diagrams show the appearance of the sky when certain events take place. However, the exact positions of celestial objects and their separations greatly depend on the observer's position on Earth. When the Moon is one of the objects involved, because it is relatively close to Earth, there may be very significant changes from one location to another. Close approaches between planets or between a planet and a star are less affected by changes of location, which may thus be ignored.

The diagrams showing the appearance of the sky are drawn at latitude 35°S and longitude 150°E (approximately that of Sydney, Australia), so will be approximately correct for much of Australia. However, for an observer farther north (say Brisbane or Darwin), a planet or star listed as being north of the Moon will appear even farther north, whereas one south of the Moon will appear closer to it – or may even be hidden (occulted) by it. For an observer at a latitude greater than 35°S (such as in New Zealand), there will be corresponding changes in the opposite direction: For a star or planet south of the Moon the separation will increase, and for one north of the Moon the separation will decrease. For example, on 8 September 2019 during the occultation of Saturn (pages 72 and 73), the apparent path of the planet will be farther south for observers in Perth, Western Australia, than for observers in Darwin, Northern Territory.

Ideally, details should be calculated for each individual observer, but this is obviously impractical. In fact, positions and separations are actually calculated for a theoretical observer located at the centre of the Earth.

So the details given regarding the positions of the various bodies should be used as a guide to their location. A similar situation arises with the times that are shown. These are calculated according to certain technical criteria, which need not concern us here. However, they do not necessarily indicate the exact time when two bodies are closest together. Similarly, dates and times are given, even if they fall in daylight, when the objects are likely to be completely invisible. However, such times do give an indication that the objects concerned will be in the same general area of the sky during both the preceding, and the following nights.

Key to the symbols used on the monthy star maps.

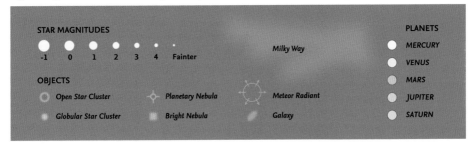

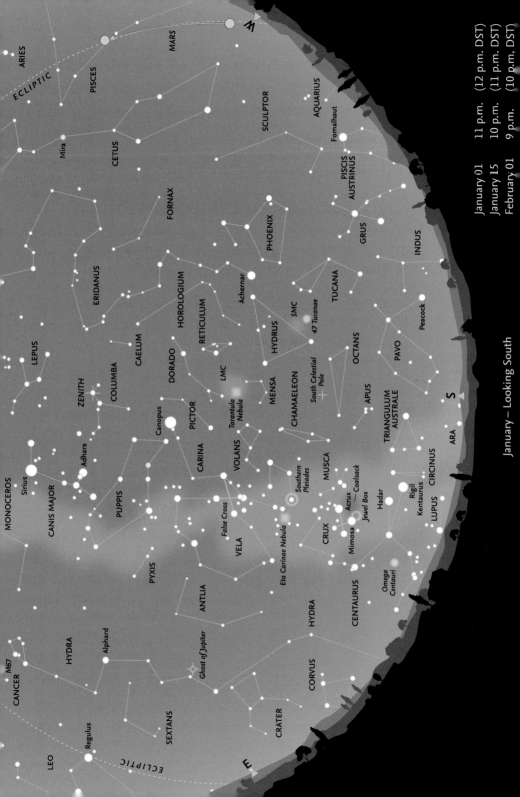

January — Looking South

ARIES
ECLIPTIC
PISCES
MARS
Mira
CETUS
SCULPTOR
AQUARIUS
Fomalhaut
PISCIS
AUSTRINUS
FORNAX
PHOENIX
GRUS
INDUS
ERIDANUS
Achernar
HOROLOGIUM
RETICULUM
HYDRUS
SMC
47 Tucanae
TUCANA
CAELUM
LEPUS
DORADO
LMC
MENSA
CHAMAELEON
OCTANS
PAVO
Peacock
COLUMBA
ZENITH
Tarantula
Nebula
South Celestial
Pole
APUS
TRIANGULUM
AUSTRALE
Adhara
Canopus
PICTOR
VOLANS
MUSCA
S
Sirius
CARINA
Southern
Pleiades
Coalsack
ARA
CANIS MAJOR
False Cross
Acrux
Jewel Box
Rigil
Kentaurus
CIRCINUS
PUPPIS
VELA
Mimosa
Hadar
LUPUS
MONOCEROS
CRUX
Eta Carinae Nebula
PYXIS
Omega
Centauri
CENTAURUS
ANTLIA
CANCER M67
Ghost of Jupiter
HYDRA
Alphard
HYDRA
CORVUS
SEXTANS
LEO
Regulus
CRATER
ECLIPTIC
E

January 01   11 p.m.   (12 p.m. DST)
January 15   10 p.m.   (11 p.m. DST)
February 01   9 p.m.   (10 p.m. DST)

January – Looking South

Crux is now quite prominent as it rises in the east, and even **Rigil Kentaurus** and **Hadar** (α and β Centauri), although low, are becoming easier to see. The whole of **Carina** is visible, with both the **Eta Carinae Nebula** and the **Southern Pleiades** between Crux and the **False Cross** of stars from the constellations of Carina and **Vela. Canopus** (α Carinae) is high in the south, roughly three-quarters of the way from the horizon to the zenith. Also in the south, but slightly lower, is the **Large Magellanic Cloud. Achernar** (α Eridani) is prominent between the constellations of **Hydrus** and **Phoenix.** The **Small Magellanic Cloud** and **47 Tucanae** are well-placed for observation alongside Hydrus. **Fomalhaut** (α Piscis Austrini) may be glimpsed low on the horizon towards the west as may **Peacock** (α Pavonis) farther towards the south.

Meteors

The year does not start well for southern meteor observers. The **Centaurids** (active late January to February) have low maximum rates, as do the **Gamma Normids** (February to March). Only with the **Pi Puppids** (maximum April 23) is there any likelihood of a higher rate of about 40, although even that is rare. The Southern **Delta Aquariids** (maximum July 29–30) have a rate of about 20 per hour, as do the **Orionids** (maximum October 21–22). Only with the **Leonids** (maximum November 17–18) is there a chance of a high rate of around 100, but it is likely to be about 15 per hour. The **Phoenicids** in November-December (maximum December 2) are unpredictable, but may show strong activity. The last major shower of the year, the **Geminids** (maximum December 13–14) finally achieves a rate of about 120 per hour.

The constellation of Orion dominates the northern sky during this period of the year, and is a useful starting point for recognizing other constellations in the area (see next page). Here, orange Betelgeuse, blue-white Rigel and the pinkish Orion Nebula are prominent (south is up).

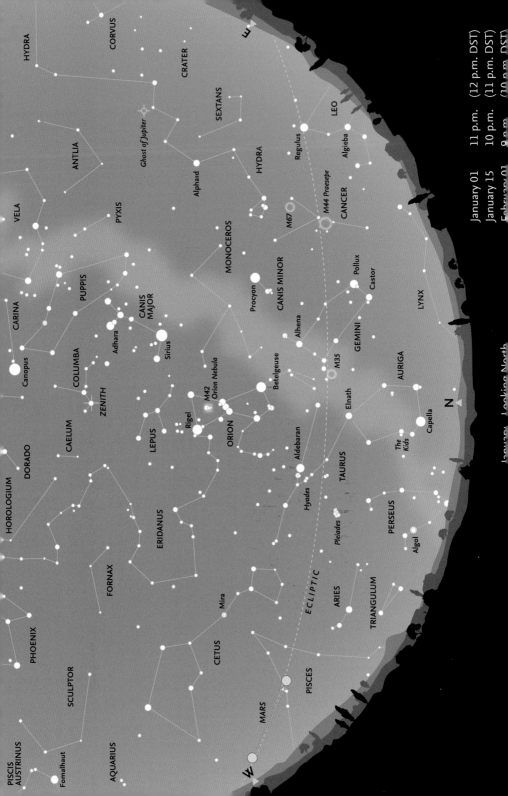

CORVUS
HYDRA
CRATER
SEXTANS
CRATER
Ghost of Jupiter
ANTLIA
Alphard
HYDRA
LEO
Regulus
Algieba
VELA
PYXIS
MONOCEROS
M44 Praesepe
M67
CANCER
PUPPIS
CARINA
CANIS
MAJOR
Adhara
Sirius
Procyon
CANIS MINOR
Pollux
Castor
LYNX
COLUMBA
Canopus
ZENITH
M42
Orion Nebula
Betelgeuse
Alhena
M35
GEMINI
CAELUM
LEPUS
Rigel
ORION
Aldebaran
Elnath
AURIGA
DORADO
HOROLOGIUM
TAURUS
The
Kids
Capella
N
FORNAX
ERIDANUS
Hyades
PERSEUS
PHOENIX
Mira
Pleiades
Algol
SCULPTOR
CETUS
ARIES
ECLIPTIC
TRIANGULUM
PISCIS
AUSTRINUS
Fomalhaut
AQUARIUS
PISCES
MARS
W

January, Looking North

January 01   11 p.m.   (12 p.m. DST)
January 15   10 p.m.   (11 p.m. DST)
February 01   9 p.m.   (10 p.m. DST)

January – Looking North

At this time of year the northern sky is dominated by **Orion**. This is the most prominent constellation during the summer months, when it is visible at some time during the night. (A photograph of Orion appears on page 21.) It has a highly distinctive shape, with a line of three stars that form the 'Belt'. To most observers, the bright star at the northeastern corner of the constellation, **Betelgeuse** (α Orionis), shows a reddish tinge, in contrast to the brilliant bluish-white colour of the bright star at the southwestern corner, **Rigel** (β Orionis). The three stars of the belt lie directly south of the celestial equator. A vertical line of three 'stars' forms the 'Sword' that hangs to the south of the Belt. With good viewing conditions, the central 'star' appears as a hazy spot, even to the naked eye. This is actually the **Orion Nebula**. Binoculars will reveal the four stars of the '**Trapezium**', which illuminate the nebula.

The line of Orion's Belt points up to the northwest towards **Taurus** (the Bull) and above orange-tinted **Aldebaran** (α Tauri). Close to Aldebaran, there is a conspicuous 'V' of stars, pointing down to the southwest, called the **Hyades** cluster. (Despite appearances, Aldebaran is not part of the cluster.) Farther along, the same line from Orion

The constellation of Gemini. The two brightest stars are Pollux and Castor, visible on the right-hand side of the photograph (south is up).

passes above a bright cluster of stars, the **Pleiades**, or Seven Sisters. Even the smallest pair of binoculars reveals this cluster to be a beautiful group of bluish-white stars. The two most conspicuous of the other stars in Taurus lie directly above Orion, and form an elongated triangle with Aldebaran. The northernmost, **Elnath** (β Tauri), was once considered to be part of the constellation of Auriga.

The Moon's phases for January

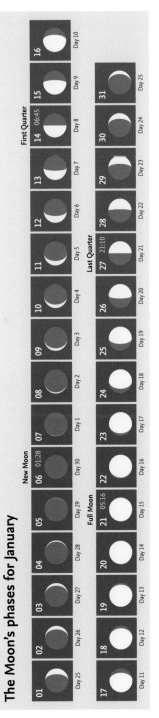

January – Moon and Planets

The Earth

The Earth reaches perihelion (the closest point to the Sun in its annual orbit) on 3 January 2019, at 05:20 Universal Time. Its distance is then 0.9833 AU (147,099,586 km).

The Moon

On January 3 the Moon is close to Jupiter in Scorpius. On January 6 at New Moon there is a partial solar eclipse, visible from the region of the northwestern Pacific and northeastern Asia. On January 17, the Moon is close to **Aldebaran** in **Taurus**. A total lunar eclipse occurs at Full Moon on January 21, visible from a wide area of the Pacific, including Australia and eastern Asia. The Moon passes close to **Regulus** in **Leo** on January 23.

The planets

Mercury is too close to the Sun to be readily visible this month. **Venus** reaches greatest elongation west (47°) on January 6, when its magnitude is -4.6. **Mars** moves across the constellation of **Pisces**, fading from mag. 0.5 to 0.9 over the month. **Jupiter** is fairly bright (mag. -1.9 to -1.8) and in **Ophiuchus**, seen only in the early morning. **Saturn** is in **Sagittarius**, too near the Sun to be visible. **Uranus** (mag. 5.8) is on the border of **Pisces** and **Aries**. **Neptune** (mag. 7.9) is in **Aquarius**, where it remains throughout the year.

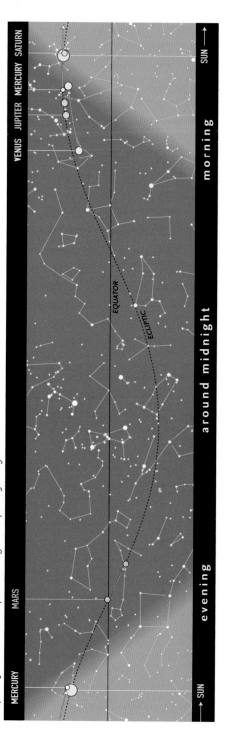

The path of the Sun and the planets along the ecliptic in January.

Calendar for January

01	21:48	Venus 1.3°S of Moon
02	05:50	Saturn in conjunction with Sun
03	05:20	Earth at perihelion (147,099,586 km = 0.9833 AU)
03	07:35	Jupiter 3.1°S of Moon
04	17:40	Mercury 2.7°S of Moon
05	18:42	Saturn 0.9°S of Moon
06	01:28	New Moon
06	01:41	Partial solar eclipse (NW Pacific, NE Asia)
06	04:59	Venus at greatest elongation (47°W, mag. −4.6)
09	04:29	Moon at apogee (406,117 km)
12	19:47	Mars 5.3°N of Moon
14	06:45	First Quarter
15	21:00 *	Venus 7.9°N of Antares
17	18:20	Aldebaran 1.6°S of Moon
21	05:12	Total lunar eclipse (Pacific, Australia, E. Asia)
21	05:16	Full Moon
21	20:00	Moon at perigee (357,342 km)
22	15:10	Venus 2.4°N of Jupiter
23	01:41	Regulus 2.5°S of Moon
27	21:10	Last Quarter
28–Feb.21		Centaurid meteor shower
30	02:46	Mercury superior conjunction
30	23:54	Jupiter 3°S of Moon
31	17:36	Venus 0.1°S of Moon

*These objects are close together for an extended period around this time.

Morning 5 a.m. (DST)

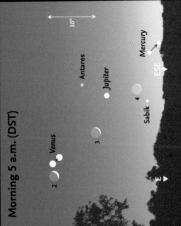

January 2–4 • The Moon passes Venus and Jupiter. Mercury is close to the horizon and may be lost in dawn.

Morning 4 a.m. (DST)

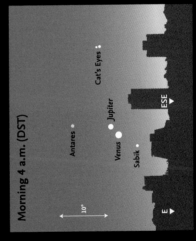

January 23 • Venus and Jupiter with Antares, Sabik and the Cat's Eyes (λ and υ Sco), low in the east.

Evening 11:30 p.m. (DST)

January 17 • The Moon is between Aldebaran and the Pleiades. Elnath is farther north.

Morning 5 a.m. (DST)

January 31 • The Moon with Antares, Jupiter, Venus and Sabik about 30 degrees above the eastern horizon.

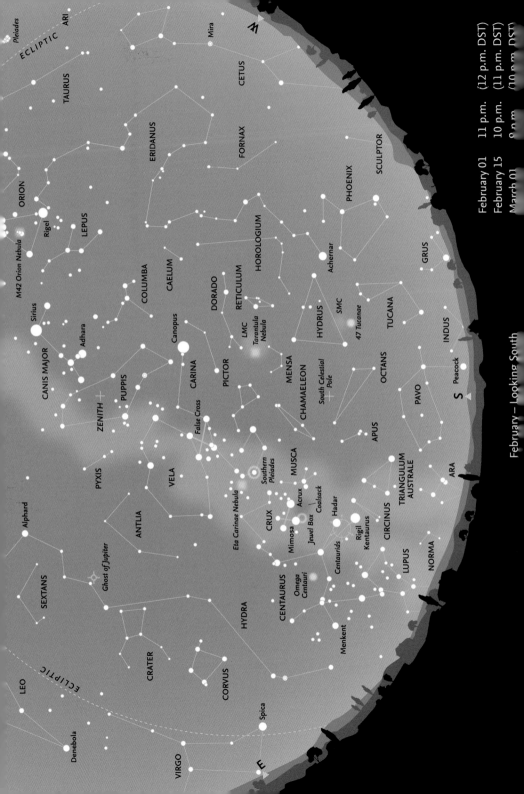

February 01   11 p.m.   (12 p.m. DST)
February 15   10 p.m.   (11 p.m. DST)
March 01   9 p.m.   (10 p.m. DST)

February – Looking South

February – Looking South

The whole of **Centaurus** is now clear of the horizon in the south-east, where, below it, the constellation of **Lupus** is beginning to be visible. **Triangulum Australe** is now higher in the sky and easier to see. Both **Crux** and the **False Cross** are also higher and more visible. The **Large Magellanic Cloud** (LMC) and brilliant Canopus are now almost due south, with the constellation of Puppis at the zenith. Both **Hydrus** and the **Small Magellanic Cloud** (SMC) are lower in the sky, as is **Phoenix**, which is much closer to the horizon in the west. Next to it, the constellation of **Tucana** is also lower although the globular cluster **47 Tucanae** remains readily visible as does **Achernar** (α Eridani). The constellation of **Grus** and bright **Fomalhaut** (α Piscis Austrini) have disappeared below the horizon. **Peacock** (α Pavonis) is skimming the horizon in the south and is not easily seen at any time in the night.

Meteors

The **Centaurid** shower (which actually consists of two separate streams (the **Alpha** and **Beta Centaurids**), with both radiants lying near α and β Centauri), continues in February, reaching a low maximum (around 5 meteors per hour) on February 8, when the Moon is a waxing crescent. Another weak shower, the **Gamma Normids**, begins to be active in late February (February 25), but the meteors are difficult to differentiate from sporadics. It reaches its weak (but sharp) maximum in March.

Parts of Carina and Vela. The 'False Cross' is indicated with blue lines. The red blurry spot near the bottom left corner is the Eta (η) Carinae Nebula. To the right, and a little lower, is an open cluster that surrounds Theta (θ) Carinae. This cluster (IC 2602) is also known as the Southern Pleiades.

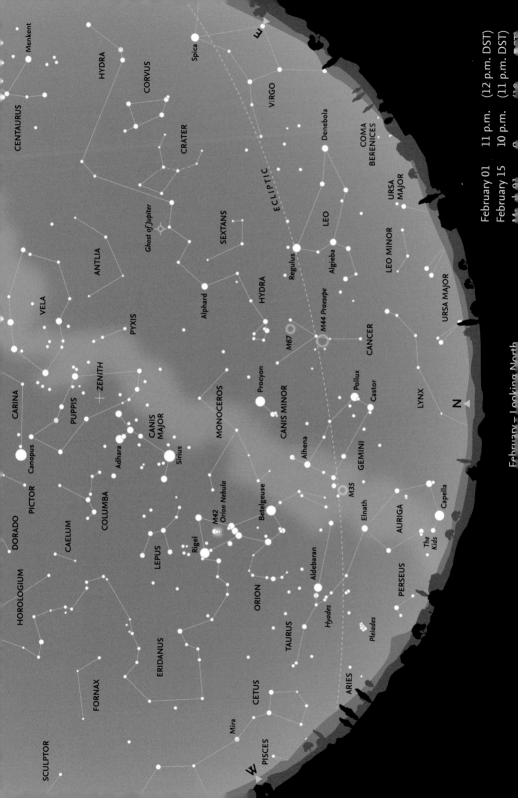

February 01   11 p.m.   (12 p.m. DST)
February 15   10 p.m.   (11 p.m. DST)

February – Looking North

February – Looking North

The constellation of *Gemini*, with the pair of stars *Castor* and *Pollux* (α and β Geminorum) is now due north. Pollux is higher in the sky (farther towards the zenith), and above it is *Procyon* (α Canis Minoris), half-way to the zenith. Still higher is *Sirius*, the brightest star in the sky and the constellation of *Canis Major*. The faint constellation of *Cancer*, with its most noticeable feature, the cluster *Praesepe*, lies to the east of Gemini. Above it, and directly east of Procyon, is the distinctive asterism forming the head of *Hydra*, the whole of which constellation is now visible stretching across the sky towards the east. The constellation of *Taurus*, with orange *Aldebaran* (α Tauri) is still clearly seen in the west. By contrast, *Auriga* is much lower towards the horizon and brilliant *Capella* (α Aurigae) is extremely low and visible only early in the night. The faintest stretch of the Milky Way runs from Auriga in the northwest up towards the zenith, passing through Gemini and the indistinct constellation of *Monoceros*. In the northeast, the zodiacal constellation of *Leo* and bright *Regulus* (α Leonis) are clearly seen.

The constellation of Cancer. Just below the centre is the open star cluster M44 (Praesepe), sometimes called the 'Beehive'. The two bright stars near the left side are Castor and Pollux, and the head of Hydra may be found in the upper right (south is up).

The Moon's phases for February

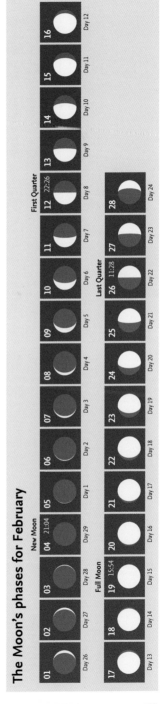

						New Moon		
01	02	03	04 21:04	05	06	07	08	09
Day 26	Day 27	Day 28	Day 29	Day 1	Day 2	Day 3	Day 4	Day 5
			Full Moon					

			First Quarter				
10	11	12 22:26	13	14	15	16	
Day 6	Day 7	Day 8	Day 9	Day 10	Day 11	Day 12	
Last Quarter							

17	18	19 15:54	20	21	22	23	24
Day 13	Day 14	Day 15	Day 16	Day 17	Day 18	Day 19	Day 20

25	26 11:28	27	28				
Day 21	Day 22	Day 23	Day 24				

February – Moon and Planets

The Moon

The Moon is at its most distant apogee on February 5. It is 0.7°N of **Saturn** on February 2 and is 1.2°S of Venus later that day. On February 14, it is 1.7°N of **Aldebaran**, and five days later (February 19) is 2.4°N of **Regulus**. It is 2.5°N of **Jupiter** on February 27.

Occultations

Of the bright stars near the ecliptic that may be occulted by the Moon (**Aldebaran, Antares, Pollux, Regulus** and **Spica**), none are occulted in 2019. (There are occultations of **Saturn** in 2019, visible from the southern hemisphere, but not of any other planets.)

The planets

Mercury is lost in daylight, and although it reaches greatest eastern elongation on February 27, is too low to be readily visible. **Venus** is visible in the morning sky, rapidly moving closer to the Sun and fading slightly from mag. -4.3 to -4.1 over the month. **Mars** (at mag. 0.9 to 1.2) moves from **Pisces** into **Aries** in mid-month. **Jupiter** (mag. -1.9 to -2.0) is slowly moving east in **Ophiuchus**. **Saturn**, in **Sagittarius**, is also moving very slowly eastwards at mag. 0.6. **Uranus** (mag. 5.8) is in **Aries**, just inside the border with **Pisces. Neptune** (mag. 7.9) remains in **Aquarius**.

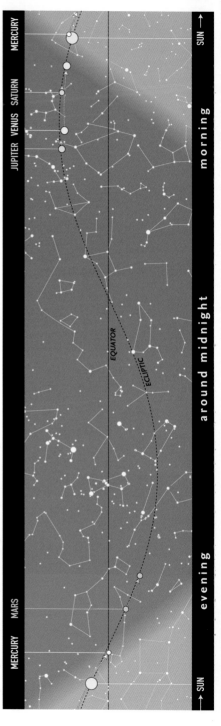

The path of the Sun and the planets along the ecliptic in February.

Calendar for February

02	07:18	Saturn 0.7°S of Moon
02	21:27	Venus 1.2°N of Moon
04	21:04	New Moon
05	07:02	Mercury 6.1°N of Moon
05	09:29	Moon at apogee (farthest of year, 406,555 km)
07	12:37	Mercury 8.4°N of Moon
08		Centaurid shower maximum
10	16:19	Mars 6.1°N of Moon
12	22:26	First Quarter
14	02:29	Aldebaran 1.7°S of Moon
18	14:16	Venus 1.1°N of Saturn
19	09:03	Moon at perigee (closest of year, 356,761 km)
19	13:08	Regulus 2.4°S of Moon
19	15:54	Full Moon
26	11:28	Last Quarter
25–Mar.22		Gamma Normid meteor shower
27	01:25	Mercury at greatest elongation (18.1°E, mag. –0.5)
27	14:16	Jupiter 2.5°S of Moon

Morning 5:30 a.m. (DST)

February 1–3 • The Moon passes Venus, and Saturn, shortly before sunrise. Nunki and Kaus Australis are nearby.

After midnight 2 a.m. (DST)

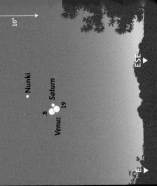

February 20 • The Full Moon is between Regulus and Algieba. Denebola is farther east.

Morning 5 a.m. (DST)

February 18–19 • Venus passes Saturn with Nunki nearby.

Early morning 3 a.m. (DST)

February 26–28 • Around Last Quarter, the Moon passes Antares, Sabik and Jupiter, high in the east.

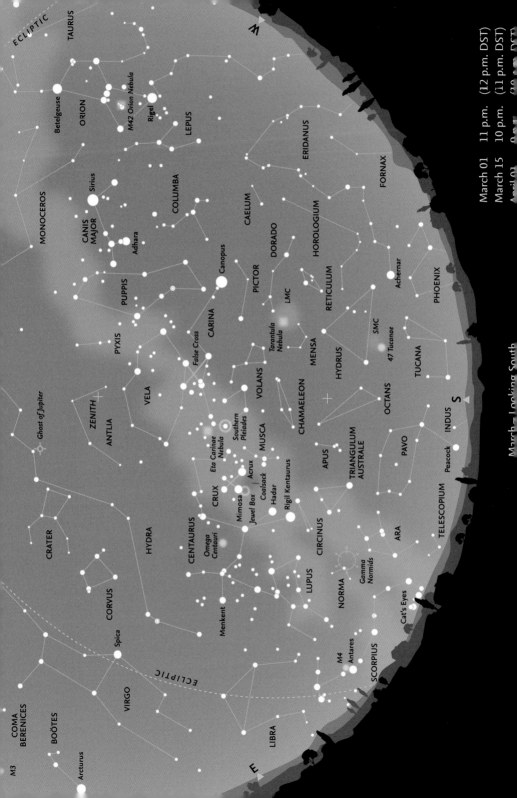

March – Looking South

March 01 11 p.m. (12 p.m. DST)
March 15 10 p.m. (11 p.m. DST)
April 01   9 p.m.   (10 p.m. DST)

March – Looking South

The dark area left of the centre of the image is the Coalsack. Above it lie the stars that form the constellation of Crux, the Southern Cross. The constellation of Musca is in the bottom half of the image. Near the upper right corner is the Eta Carinae Nebula, with the Southern Pleiades just below it (north is up).

In March, the Sun crosses the celestial equator on Wednesday, March 20, when day and night are of almost exactly equal length, and the southern autumn is considered to have begun. (The hours of daylight and darkness change most rapidly around the equinoxes, in March and September.)

Scorpius is beginning to become visible in the eastern sky, but above it, the whole of the constellation of **Lupus** is now easy to see. The magnificent globular cluster of **Omega Centauri** is now readily visible, north-east of **Crux**. The **Coalsack** and the denser region of the Milky Way in **Carina**, together with the **Eta Carinae Nebula** and the **Southern Pleiades** are well placed for observation. The **False Cross** on the **Carina/Vela** border is now high in the sky, between the South Celestial Pole and the zenith. Brilliant **Canopus** (α Carinae) is only slightly lower toward the west, above the **Large Magellanic Cloud** (LMC) and the striking **Tarantula Nebula. Achernar** (α Eridani), the **Small Magellanic Cloud** (SMC) and **47 Tucanae** are considerably lower, but still clear of the horizon. **Peacock** (α Pavonis) remains low, skimming the horizon, just east of south. **Orion** is now visibly getting lower in the west, and is being followed by **Sirius** and **Canis Major**.

Meteors

The only significant meteor shower in March is the **Gamma Normids,** which have a low rate, and are thus difficult to differentiate from sporadics. However, they exhibit a very sharp peak a day or so on either side of maximum on March 13 (when the Moon is a waxing crescent that may cause some interference). The faint constellation of **Norma** rises early in the night, but most meteors are likely to be seen (away from the radiant) in the hours after midnight.

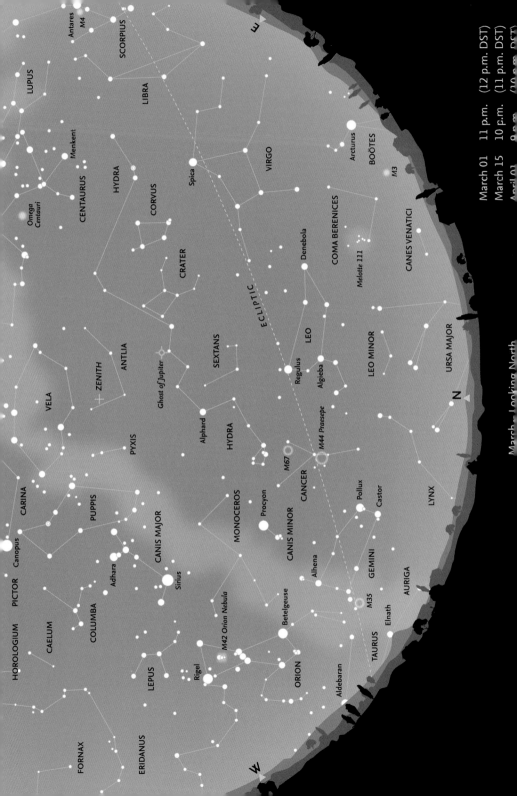

March — Looking North

March 01   11 p.m.   (12 p.m. DST)
March 15   10 p.m.   (11 p.m. DST)

March – Looking North

Almost due north is the constellation of *Leo*, with the 'backward question mark' (or 'Sickle') of bright stars forming the head of the mythological lion. *Regulus* (α Leonis) – the 'dot' of the 'question mark' or the handle of the sickle and the brightest star in Leo – lies very close to the ecliptic and is one of the few first-magnitude stars that may be occulted by the Moon, although none occur in 2019. To the west lies the faint constellation of *Cancer*, with the open cluster M44, or *Praesepe.* The constellations of *Gemini* and *Orion* are now getting low in the west, but above them, both *Procyon* in Canis Minor and the constellation of *Canis Major* remain clear to see. The whole of *Hydra* (the largest constellation) now sprawls right across the southern and eastern skies. The unremarkable constellation of *Antlia* is at the zenith. In the east, *Arcturus* (α Boötis) – the brightest star in the northern hemisphere of the sky – is becoming visible, and climbs higher during the night.

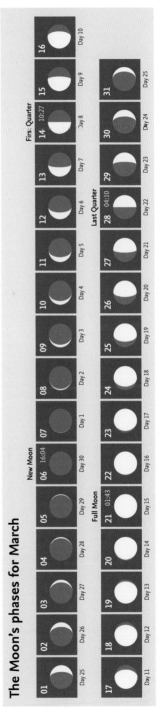

The distinctive constellation of Leo, with Regulus and 'The Sickle' on the west. Algieba (γ Leonis), north of Regulus, appearing double, is a multiple system of four stars (south is up).

The Moon's phases for March

01 Day 25	**02** Day 26	**03** Day 27	**04** Day 28	**05** Day 29 Full Moon 01:43	**06** Day 30 New Moon 16:04
07 Day 1	**08** Day 2	**09** Day 3	**10** Day 4	**11** Day 5	**12** Day 6 Last Quarter
13 Day 7	**14** Day 8 First Quarter 10:27	**15** Day 9	**16** Day 10		
17 Day 11	**18** Day 12	**19** Day 13	**20** Day 14	**21** Day 15	**22** Day 16
23 Day 17	**24** Day 18	**25** Day 19	**26** Day 20	**27** Day 21	**28** Day 22 Last Quarter 04:10
29 Day 23	**30** Day 24	**31** Day 25			

March – Moon and Planets

The Moon

The Moon passes close to **Venus** (just within Capricornus) in the morning sky on March 2, (the two bodies are closest later in the day in Capricornus, invisible in daylight). At New Moon, on March 6, the Moon is in **Aquarius** (as is the Sun). It is north of **Aldebaran** in **Taurus** on March 11 and **Regulus** in **Leo** on March 19. It is in **Virgo**, lying almost half-way between **Spica** and **Regulus**, at Full Moon on March 21. It passes close to **Jupiter** on March 27 and **Saturn** on both March 1 and March 29.

The planets

Mercury is lost in daylight (it passes inferior conjunction on March 15). **Venus** at mag. -4.0 is visible in the morning sky, crossing **Capricornus** into **Aquarius**, close to the Sun at the end of the month. **Mars** is an evening object, initially mag. 1.2 and in **Aries**, moves into **Taurus** and fades slightly (to mag. 1.4) by the end of the month. **Jupiter** (mag. -2.0 to -2.2) is moving slowly eastwards in Ophiuchus. **Saturn** (mag. 0.6) is also moving slowly eastwards in **Sagittarius**. **Uranus** is mag. 5.9 in **Aries**, and **Neptune** (mag. 7.9) remains in **Aquarius**.

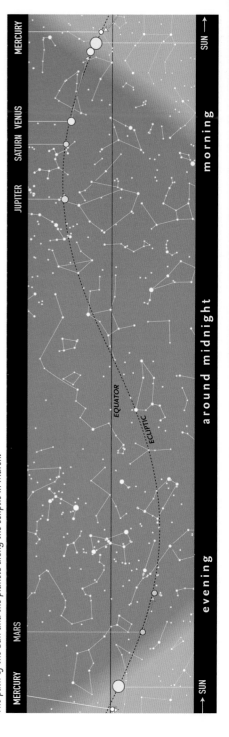

The path of the Sun and the planets along the ecliptic in March.

dar for March

18:40	Saturn 0.3°S of Moon
21:28	Venus 1.3°N of Moon
11:26	Moon at apogee (406,391 km)
16:04	New Moon
12:09	Mars 5.7°N of Moon
	Gamma Normid shower maximum
11:13	Aldebaran 2°S of Moon
10:27	First Quarter
01:47	Mercury at inferior conjunction
00:59	Regulus 2.5°S of Moon
19:48	Moon at perigee (359,377 km)
21:58	Southern autumn equinox
01:43	Full Moon
03:28	Jupiter 2°S of Moon
04:10	Last Quarter
06:11	Saturn 0.1°N of Moon
	Summer Time begins (Europe)
04:04	Mars 3.2°S of Pleiades

Morning 5 a.m. (DST)

Nunki
Saturn
Venus

March 1–4 • *The Moon passes Nunki, Saturn and Venus. On March 4 it is probably lost in the dawn.*

Evening 8 p.m. (DST)

Aldebaran
Pleiades
Mars

March 11–13 • *The Moon passes Mars, the Pleiades and Aldebaran, which is slightly brighter than Mars.*

Early morning 3 a.m. (DST)

Antares
Cat's Eyes
Sabik
Jupiter

March 26–28 • *The Moon passes Antares, Sabik and*

Morning 5 a.m. (DST)

Nunki
Saturn

March 29–30 • *The Moon in the company of Nunki*

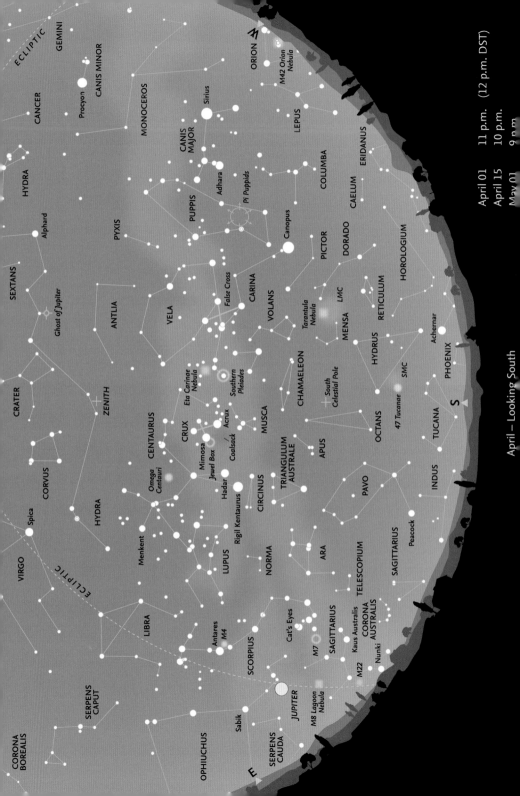

April – Looking South

April 01   11 p.m.   (12 p.m. DST)
April 15   10 p.m.
May 01   9 p.m.

April – Looking South

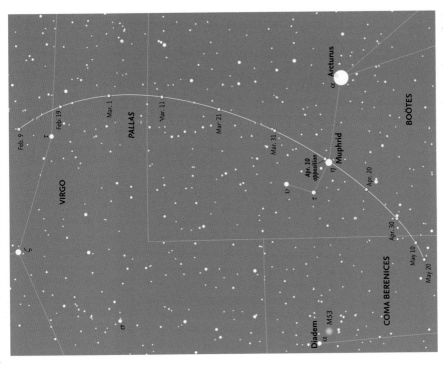

The path of minor planet Pallas (2) which is at opposition (mag. 7.9) on April 10. Background stars are shown down to magnitude 8.5 (south is up).

Daylight Saving Time ends in both Australia and New Zealand on Sunday, April 7 with the arrival of autumn. *Crux* is now high in the south, with the two brightest stars of *Centaurus* (α and β Centauri) to its east. West of Crux, both the *Southern Pleiades* and the *Eta Carinae Nebula* are clearly seen, two-thirds of the way towards the zenith. Farther west, the *False Cross* is beginning to decline towards the horizon. *Canopus* (α Carinae) is even lower, and *Orion* has now disappeared below the horizon. *Canis Major* and brilliant *Sirius* are also descending in the west. *Achernar* (α Eridani) is skimming the southern horizon, but *Peacock* (α Pavonis) is now slightly higher and more easily visible. Although the *LMC* is roughly as high as the South Celestial Pole, the *SMC* and *47 Tucanae* are rather low (but still visible) in the south. In the east, the whole of *Scorpius* is now well clear of the horizon with the constellation of *Libra* preceding it along the ecliptic. The dense regions of the Milky Way in *Sagittarius* become visible later in the night.

Meteors

Two meteor showers, in particular, occur in April. The *Pi Puppid* shower begins on April 15, but conditions are not particularly favourable in 2019, with Full Moon on April 19, and shower maximum on April 23, when the Moon is 18–19 days old (waning gibbous). The hourly rate is variable but the meteors tend to be faint. The parent body is the comet 26P/Grigg-Skjellerup. A second, more prolific, shower, the *Eta Aquariids*, begins at Full Moon on April 19, and continues into May.

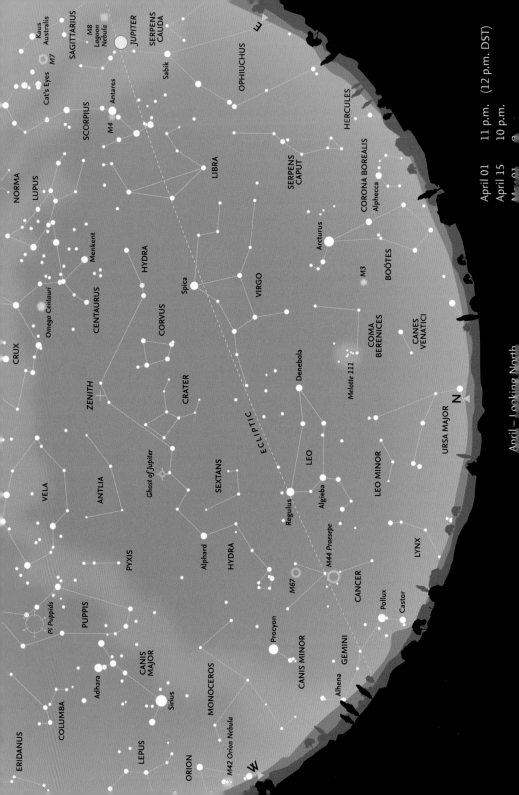

April – Looking North

April 01   11 p.m.   (12 p.m. DST)
April 15   10 p.m.

April – Looking North

Leo is the most prominent constellation in the southern sky in April, and vaguely looks like the creature after which it is named. *Gemini*, with *Castor* and *Pollux*, is low on the horizon in the west, and *Cancer* lies between the two constellations. To the east of Leo, the whole of *Virgo*, with *Spica* (α Virginis) its brightest star, is clearly visible, with the constellation of *Libra* farther east along the ecliptic. Above Leo and Virgo, the complete length of *Hydra* is visible, with *Alphard* (α Hydrae) forming a prominent triangle with *Regulus* and *Procyon* in *Canis Minor*. High in the sky, the two small constellations of *Crater* and the rather brighter *Corvus* lie between Hydra and Virgo.

Boötes and *Arcturus* are prominent in the northeastern sky, together with the circlet of *Corona Borealis*, close to the horizon. Between Leo and Boötes lies the constellation of *Coma Berenices*, notable for being the location of the open cluster Melotte 111 and the Coma Cluster of galaxies (Abell 1656). There are about 1000 galaxies in this cluster, which is located near the North Galactic Pole, where we are looking out of the plane of the Galaxy and are thus able to see deep into space. Only

A very large, and frequently ignored, open star cluster, Melotte 111, also known as the Coma Cluster, is readily visible in the northen sky during April and May (south is up).

about ten of the brightest galaxies in the Coma Cluster are visible with the largest amateur telescopes.

The Moon's phases for April

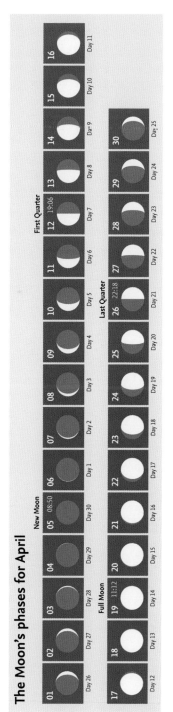

April – Moon and Planets

The Moon

At New Moon on April 5, the Moon is in *Cetus*, below the Sun, which lies in *Pisces*. On April 9 it is visible in the western sky, north of *Aldebaran* in *Taurus*. On April 15 it passes *Regulus* in *Leo*. At Full Moon, on April 19, it is in *Virgo*, not far from *Spica*. On April 23, the Moon passes close to *Jupiter* and then *Saturn* on April 25.

The planets

Mercury begins in *Aquarius* and rapidly moves to greatest western elongation on April 11. *Venus* also begins the month in Aquarius, at mag. -3.8, but then moves into the dawn twilight. Both planets are too low to be readily visible. *Mars*, in the evening sky, initially mag. 1.4, fades slightly to mag.1.6 as it moves west in *Taurus* over the month. *Jupiter*, moving slowly in *Ophiuchus*, brightens slightly from mag. -2.2 to -2.4. and *Saturn* is in *Sagittarius* at mag. 0.6—0.5. Both planets are readily visible later in the night. *Uranus* is in Aries at mag. 5.9 and *Neptune* in *Aquarius* at mag. 8.0. Both planets are invisible in the daytime sky. Minor planet *Pallas* (2) comes to opposition in *Boötes* on April 10 at mag. 7.9 (see page 39).

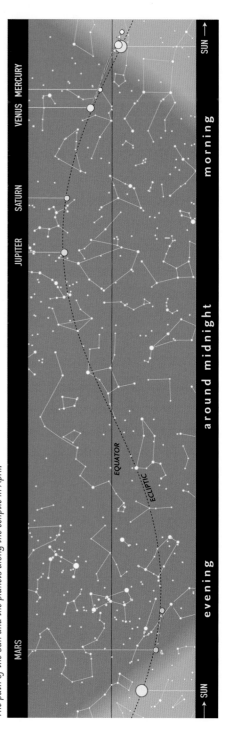

The path of the Sun and the planets along the ecliptic in April.

1	00:14	Moon at apogee (405,577 km)
2	04:17	Venus 2.7°N of Moon
3	23:01	Mercury 3.6°N of Moon
5	08:50	New Moon
6	22:00 *	Mars 6.5°N of Aldebaran
7		End of Daylight Saving Time (Australia & New Zealand)
9	07:40	Mars 5°N of Moon
9	16:43	Aldebaran 2.2°S of Moon
10	01:17	Pallas at opposition (mag. 7.9)
11	19:42	Mercury at greatest elongation (27.7°W, mag. 0.3)
12	19:06	First Quarter
15–28		Pi Puppid meteor shower
15	01:08	Aldebaran 6.5°N of Mars
15	09:22	Regulus 2.7°S of Moon
16	19:03	Mercury 4.3°S of Venus
16	22:05	Moon at perigee (364,205 km)
19–May 26		Eta Aquariid meteor shower
19	11:12	Full Moon
23		Pi Puppid shower maximum
23	11:35	Jupiter 1.6°S of Moon
25	14:27	Saturn 0.4°N of Moon
26	22:18	Last Quarter
28	18:20	Moon at apogee (404,582 km)

These objects are close together for an extended period around this time.

Evening 6:30 p.m.

April 9 · The Moon with Aldebaran, Mars, and the Pleiades low in the northwest.

Evening 8 p.m.

April 11–13 · The waxing crescent Moon passes Alhena and the twin stars Castor and Pollux. Betelgeuse is farther west.

Evening 7 p.m.

April 15 · The waxing gibbous Moon is between Regulus and Algieba.

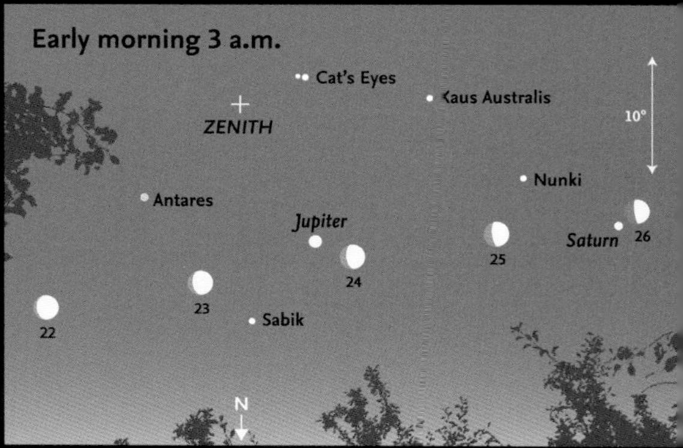

Early morning 3 a.m.

April 22–26 · The waning gibbous Moon is close to the zenith when it passes Antares, Sabik, Jupiter, Nunki, and Saturn.

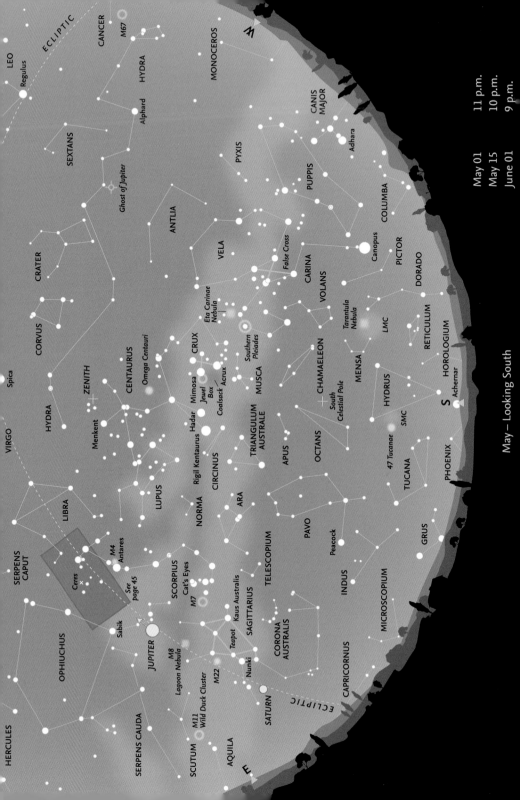

May – Looking South

11 p.m.   May 01
10 p.m.   May 15
9 p.m.   June 01

May – Looking South

In the west, **Canis Major** has set below the horizon, and **Canopus** (α Carinae) and **Puppis** are getting rather low. The whole of **Sagittarius** is now clearly seen in the east, with **Corona Australis** beneath it and **Scorpius** higher above. **Centaurus** is fully seen high in the south, with **Crux**, the **Eta Carinae Nebula**, the **Southern Pleiades** and the **False Cross** with **Vela** along the Milky Way to the west. In the south, Achernar (α Eridani) is skimming the southern horizon and the **Small Magellanic Cloud** (SMC) is beginning to rise higher in the sky, unlike the **Large Magellanic Cloud** (LMC) which is now lower. **Pavo** and **Peacock** (α Pavonis) are now much higher and even the faint constellations of **Tucana** and **Indus** are visible between Pavo and the southwestern horizon.

Meteors

The **Eta Aquariids** are one of the two meteor showers associated with Comet 1P/Halley (the other being the **Orionids**, in October). The Eta Aquariid radiant is near the celestial equator, close to the 'Water Jar' in **Aquarius**, but the constellation is well below the horizon until late in the night (around dawn). However, meteors may still be seen in the eastern sky even when the radiant is below the horizon. There is a radiant map for the Eta Aquariids on page 16.

Their maximum in 2019, on May 6–7, occurs when the Moon is a waxing crescent, just before First Quarter, so conditions should be acceptable. Maximum hourly rate is about 55 per hour and a large proportion (about 25 per cent) of the meteors leave persistent trains.

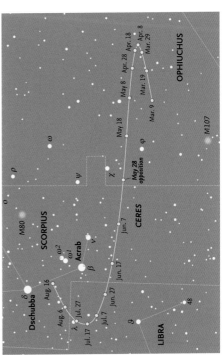

The path of minor planet Ceres (1) which comes to opposition (mag. 7.0) on May 28. Background stars are shown down to magnitude 8.5 (south is up).

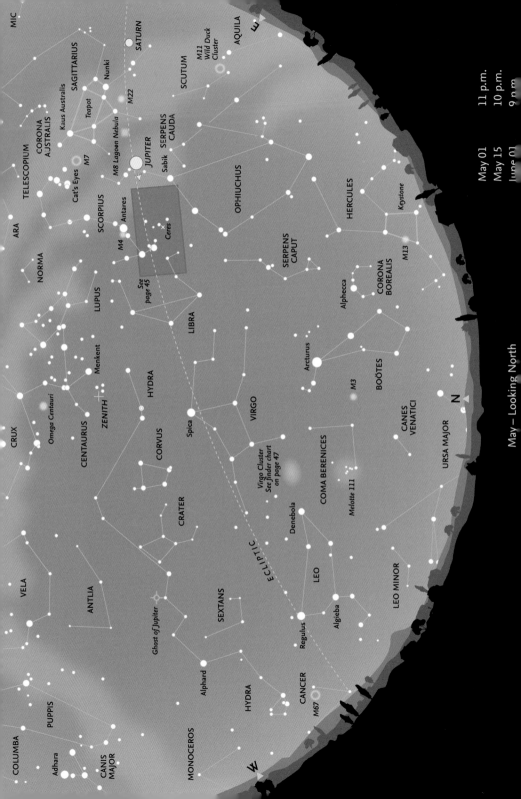

May – Looking North

May 01   11 p.m.
May 15   10 p.m.
June 01   9 p.m.

May – Looking North

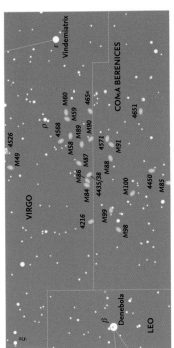

Boötes is almost due north, with brilliant, slightly orange-coloured **Arcturus** extremely prominent. The distinctive circlet of **Corona Borealis** is clearly visible to its east. The brightest star (α Coronae Borealis) is known as **Alphecca**. **Hercules** is rising in the east and becomes clearly visible later in the night. To the west of Boötes is the inconspicuous constellation of **Coma Berenices**, with the cluster **Melote 111** (see page 41) and, above it, the Virgo Cluster of galaxies (see chart).

The large constellation of **Ophiuchus** (which actually crosses the ecliptic, and is thus the 'thirteenth' zodiacal constellation) is climbing into the eastern sky. Before the constellation boundaries were formally adopted by the International Astronomical Union in 1930, the southern region of Ophiuchus was regarded as forming part of the constellation of Scorpius, which had been part of the zodiac since antiquity. **Scorpius** and brilliant, reddish **Antares** are high in the east.

Early in the night, the constellation of **Virgo**, with **Spica** (α Virginis), lies due south, with the rather faint zodiacal constellation of **Libra** to its east. Farther along the ecliptic are **Scorpius** and brilliant, reddish **Antares** (α Scorpii). In the west, the constellation of **Leo** is readily visible

A finder chart for some of the brightest galaxies in the Virgo Cluster. All stars brighter than magnitude 8.5 are shown (south is up).

now, and both **Regulus** and **Denebola** (α and β Leonis, respectively) are prominent.

Virgo contains the nearest large cluster of galaxies, which is the centre of the Local Supercluster, of which the Milky Way galaxy forms part. The Virgo Cluster contains some 2000 galaxies, the brightest of which are visible in amateur telescopes.

The Moon's phases for May

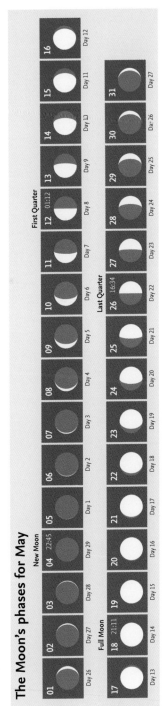

May – Moon and Planets

The Moon

New Moon occurs on May 4, when it is actually in the constellation of *Aries*, close to the border with *Cetus*. It is visible near to *Mars* on May 7 just before the planet sets in the west. It appears in *Leo*, not far from *Regulus* on May 12, at First Quarter. Full Moon is on May 18, in the constellation of *Libra*. It is close to *Jupiter* on May 20 and passes *Saturn* on May 22.

The planets

Mercury is invisible, close to the Sun, and is at superior conjunction on May 21. *Venus* is close to the horizon at dawn at the beginning of the month, but rapidly becomes invisible in daylight. *Mars* (mag. 1.6–1.7) may be glimpsed in *Taurus* in the evening twilight early in the month, but by the end of the month becomes too low as it moves into *Gemini*. *Jupiter* (mag. -2.5), and still in *Ophiuchus*, rises about 04:30 UT. *Saturn* (mag. 0.5), in *Sagittarius*, rises slightly later at about 06:00 and brightens slightly to mag. 0.3 over the month. *Uranus* is in *Aries* at mag. 5.9 and *Neptune* in *Aquarius* at mag. 7.9. The minor planet *Ceres* is at opposition (mag. 7.0) on May 28 in *Ophiuchus*, just inside the border with *Scorpius*.

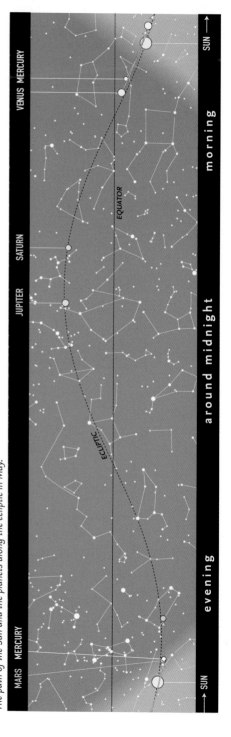

The path of the Sun and the planets along the ecliptic in May.

Calendar for May

02	11:39	Venus 3.6°N of Moon
03	06:25	Mercury 2.9°N of Moon
04	22:45	New Moon
06–07		Eta Aquariid shower maximum
06	22:20	Aldebaran 2.3°S of Moon
07	23:35	Mars 3.2°N of Moon
10	03:56	Pollux 6.3°N of Moon
12	01:12	First Quarter
12	14:44	Regulus 3°S of Moon
13	21:53	Moon at perigee (369,009 km)
16	06:37	Spica 7.7°S of Moon
18	21:11	Full Moon
19	17:05	Antares 7.9°S of Moon
20	16:54	Jupiter 1.7°S of Moon
21	13:07	Mercury at superior conjunction
22	22:14	Saturn 0.5°N of Moon
26	13:27	Moon at apogee (404,138 km)
26	16:34	Last Quarter
28	22:36	Ceres at opposition (mag. 7.0)

Evening 5:45 p.m.

May 6–9 • *The Moon passes Aldebaran (mag. 0.9), Mars (mag. 1.6) and Alhena (mag. 1.9), shortly after sunset.*

Evening 10:30 p.m.

May 12 • *The Moon is in the company of Regulus and Algieba when it sets.*

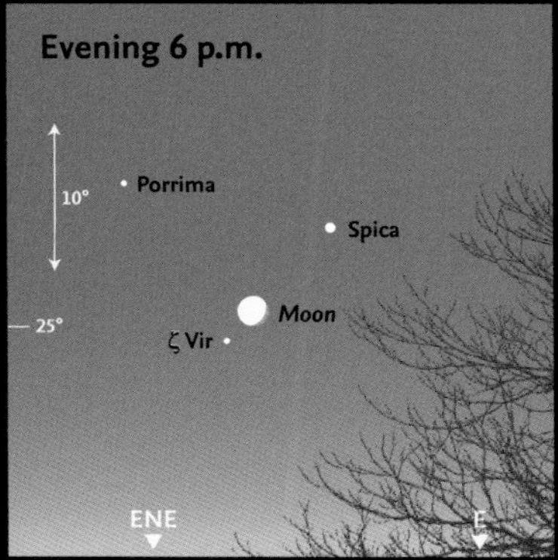

Early morning 2 a.m.

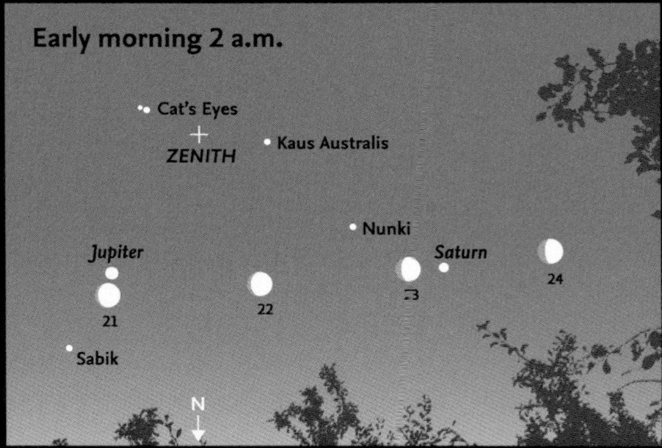

May 21–24 • *The waning gibbous Moon is very high in the north when it passes Sabik, Jupiter, Nunki and Saturn.*

Evening 6 p.m.

May 16 • *The Moon is between Spica and ζ Vir. Porrima (γ Vir) is nearby.*

MAY   49

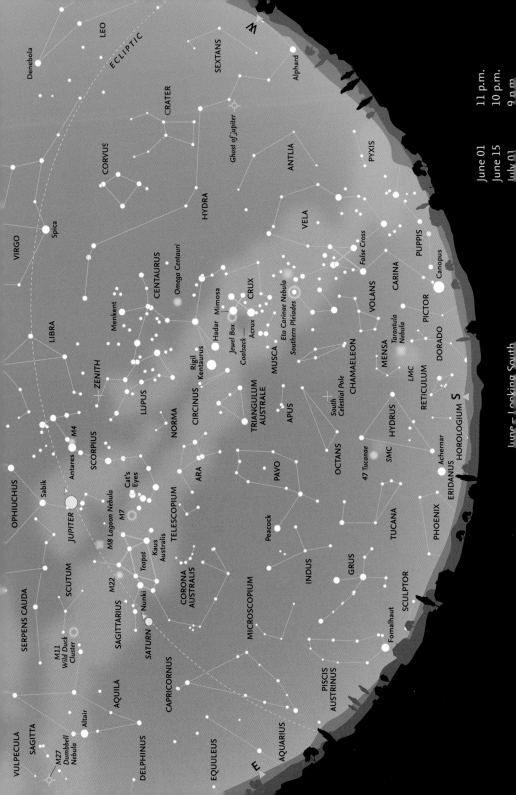

June—Looking South

June 01   11 p.m.
June 15   10 p.m.
July 01   9 p.m.

June – Looking South

Both **Canopus** (α Carinae) and **Achernar** (α Eridani) are skimming the southern horizon. Although the whole of **Carina** is visible, all of **Eridanus** (except **Achernar**) is hidden below the horizon. The **Large Magellanic Cloud** (LMC) is low, altough the **Small Magellanic Cloud** (SMC), the globular cluster, **47 Tucanae** and **Hydrus** are now rather higher. **Alphard** (α Hydrae) is on the horizon, and the constellation of **Sextans** is becoming low. However, the remainder of the long constellation of Hydra is clearly seen as are the two constellations of **Crater** and **Corvus** to its north. The **False Cross** between Carina and **Vela** is beginning to descend in the west, but Vela itself is clearly visible. The whole of both **Crux** and **Centaurus** is clearly seen, as are the magnificent globular cluster, **Omega Centauri**, and the constellation of **Lupus**, closer to the zenith. The constellation of **Triangulum Australe** is on the meridian, roughly half-way between the South Celestial Pole and the zenith. Both **Scorpius**, with brilliant, red **Antares** (α Scorpii) and **Sagittarius** are high overhead, with the faint constellation of **Corona Australis** visible below them. The whole of **Capricornus** is visible, and the constellation of **Grus** has now risen above the horizon, with the faint constellation of **Indus** between it and **Pavo**. To the east of Grus is **Piscis Austrinus**, although brilliant **Fomalhaut** (α Piscis Austrini) is only just clear of the horizon, and becomes clearly visible only later in the night and later in the month.

Omega Centauri (NGC 5139) is the largest and finest globular cluster in the sky (and in the Milky Way galaxy). It is believed to contain 10 million stars and differs in chemical composition and nature so greatly from other globulars that it may be the core of a disrupted dwarf galaxy, captured by the far more massive Galaxy.

JUNE   51

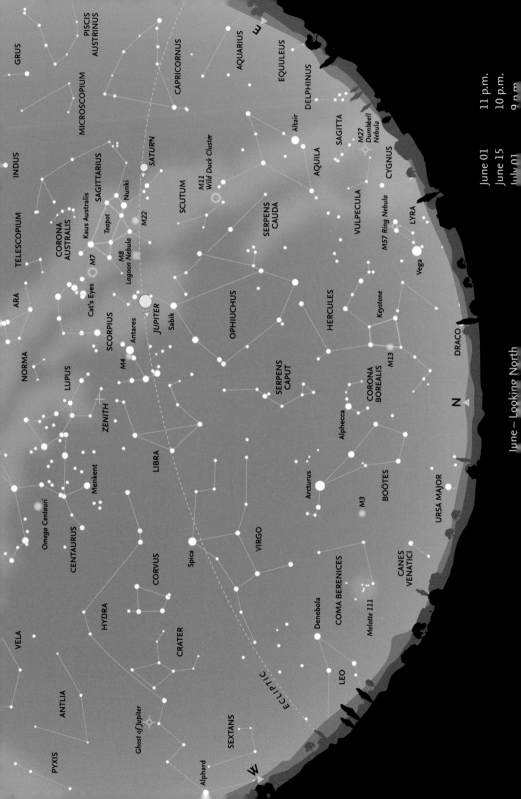

June – Looking North

June 01	11 p.m.
June 15	10 p.m.
July 01	9 p.m.

June – Looking North

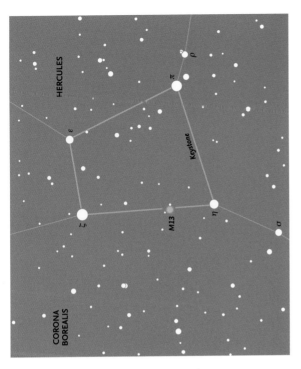

Vega in **Lyra** is just above the northeastern horizon. Closer to the meridian the whole of **Hercules** is visible including the **'Keystone'** and **M13**, widely regarded as the finest globular cluster in the northern hemisphere. The small constellation of **Corona Borealis** is almost due north. To the west of the meridian is **Boötes** and **Arcturus** (α Boötis). Much of **Leo** is now below the western horizon, but **Denebola** (β Leonis) is still visible. Higher in the sky, the whole of **Virgo** is clearly visible and, still higher, not far from the zenith is the constellation of **Libra**. To its east is **Scorpius** and reddish **Antares**. Farther along the ecliptic, both the constellations of **Sagittarius** and **Capricornus** are completely visible. Between Hercules and Sagittarius is the large constellation of **Ophiuchus** and, to its east, **Aquila** and **Altair** (α Aquilae), one of the stars of the Summer Triangle.

Finder chart for M13, the finest globular cluster in the northern sky. All stars down to magnitude 7.5 are shown (south is up).

The Moon's phases for June

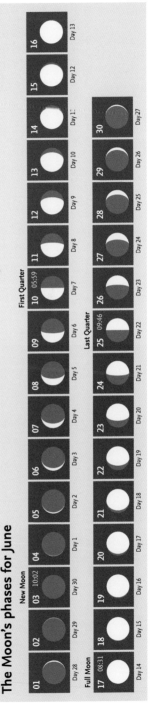

June – Moon and Planets

The Moon

New Moon is on June 3 when it is close to **Aldebaran** in **Taurus**, but the star is invisible in morning twilight. Later in the month the Moon is again near Aldebaran on June 30, but the star is now in daylight. It passes close to **Mars** on June 5, and both bodies may be glimpsed later in **Gemini** just before they set in the west. It passes **Spica** in **Virgo** in daylight on June 12 and again both bodies may be seen later in the day as they begin to set in the southwest. It is in **Ophiuchus**, above **Antares** (in **Scorpius**) on June 16 and passes close to **Jupiter** later that day. Full Moon is on June 17 (in **Ophiuchus**, near Jupiter). It passes very close to **Saturn** (in **Sagittarius**) on June 19, but the event occurs when the bodies are below the horizon. They may be seen relatively close to one another some hours later when they have risen in the east.

The planets

Mercury is initially in the daytime sky, but rapidly moves to greatest eastern elongation on June 23, when it is actually close to **Mars**, but too low to be visible after sunset. It may be possible to glimpse **Venus** (at mag. -3.9) early in the month, very low in morning twilight, but it soon moves into daylight. **Mars** is in **Gemini**, but invisible in daylight, although moving into the western evening sky. **Jupiter** is in **Ophiuchus** at mag. -2.6 and comes to opposition on June 10. **Saturn** (mag. 0.3–0.1) is in **Sagittarius**. The opposition of both planets are shown on the special chart on page 18. **Uranus** remains in Aries at mag. 5.9 and **Neptune** in **Aquarius** at mag. 7.9.

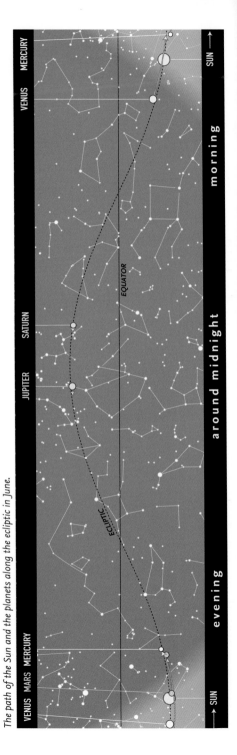

The path of the Sun and the planets along the ecliptic in June.

Calendar for June

01	18:14	Venus 3.2°N of Moon
03	06:12	Aldebaran 2.3°S of Moon
03	10:02	New Moon
04	15:41	Mercury 3.7°N of Moon
05	15:05	Mars 1.6°N of Moon
06	10:07	Pollux 6.2°N of Moon
07	23:15	Moon at perigee (368,504 km)
08	20:01	Regulus 3.2°S of Moon
10	05:59	First Quarter
10	15:28	Jupiter at opposition (mag. –2.6)
12	12:49	Spica 7.8°S of Moon
16	01:02	Antares 8°S of Moon
16	18:50	Jupiter 2°S of Moon
17	08:31	Full Moon
17	21:00 *	Venus 4.8°N of Aldebaran
18	15:00 *	Mars 0.2°S of Mercury
19	03:46	Saturn 0.4°N of Moon
21	15:54	Summer solstice
23	07:00 *	Mars 5.6°S of Pollux
23	07:50	Moon at apogee (404,548 km)
23	23:16	Mercury at greatest elongation (25.2°E, mag. 0.4)
25	09:46	Last Quarter
30	15:34	Aldebaran 2.3°S of Moon

These objects are close together for an extended
…d around this time.

Evening 5:30 p.m.

June 4–6 • The Moon passes Mercury and Mars. Mercury is very low and may be lost in the dawn.

Evening 7 p.m.

June 8–9 • The Moon passes between Regulus and Algieba. Denebola is higher and farther north.

After midnight 0:30 a.m.

June 17–20 • The Moon is again very high in the north when it passes Sabik, Jupiter, Nunki and Saturn.

Evening 5:30 p.m.

June 18 • After sunset Mercury (mag. 0.4) and Mars (mag. 1.8) are, …together…

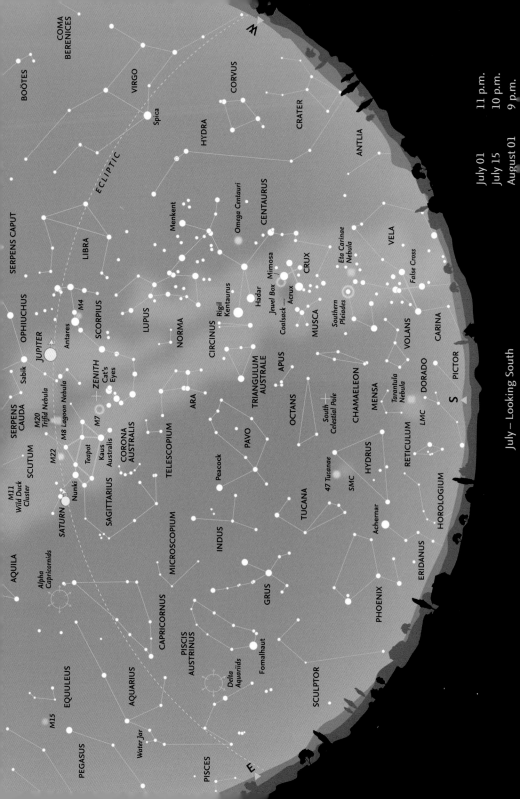

July – Looking South

July 01   11 p.m.
July 15   10 p.m.
August 01   9 p.m.

July – Looking South

The constellation of Crux is in the lower right part of the image, with the Coalsack nearby. The two bright stars near the left edge are Rigil Kentaurus (α Centauri) and Hadar (β Centauri). The fuzzy spot near the top of the image is the beautiful globular cluster Omega Centauri (see image on page 51). North is up.

Although the *Large Magellanic Cloud* (LMC) is almost due south, it is very low. Slightly farther west, the *False Cross* is nearing the horizon. Some of *Hydra* remains visible, but the constellation of *Crater* is becoming very low. *Corvus* is still easy to see. The zodiacal constellation of *Virgo* will soon be disappearing in the west. *Crux*, *Centaurus* and *Lupus* are still clearly seen, high in the sky, as is *Scorpius*, the tail of which is near the zenith. *Achernar* (α Eridani), *Hydrus*, and the *Small Magellanic Cloud* (SMC) are now higher above the horizon and easier to observe. The whole of the constellation of *Phoenix* is also now clear of the horizon. Above it are *Tucana* and, halfway to the zenith, the constellation of *Pavo*. *Grus* and *Pisces Austrinus* (with brilliant *Fomalhaut*) are now fully visible. Higher in the sky are the zodiacal constellations of *Capricornus* and *Aquarius*, and even the westernmost portion of *Pisces* is rising above the horizon.

Meteors

July brings increasing meteor activity, mainly because there are several minor radiants active in the constellations of *Capricornus* and *Aquarius*. The first shower, the *Alpha Capricornids*, active from July 11 to August 10 (peaking July 26 to August 1), does often produce very bright fireballs. The maximum rate, however, is only about 5 per hour. The parent body is Comet 169P/NEAT. The most prominent shower is probably that of the *Delta Aquariids*, which are active from around July 21 to August 23, with a peak on July 29–30, although even then the hourly rate is unlikely to reach 20 meteors per hour. In this case, the parent body is possibly Comet 96P/Machholz. This year both shower maxima occur when the Moon is a waning crescent, so observing conditions are reasonably favourable. The *Piscis Austrinids* begin on July 15 and continue until August 10, with a maximum (with a rate of about 5 per hour) on July 27–28.

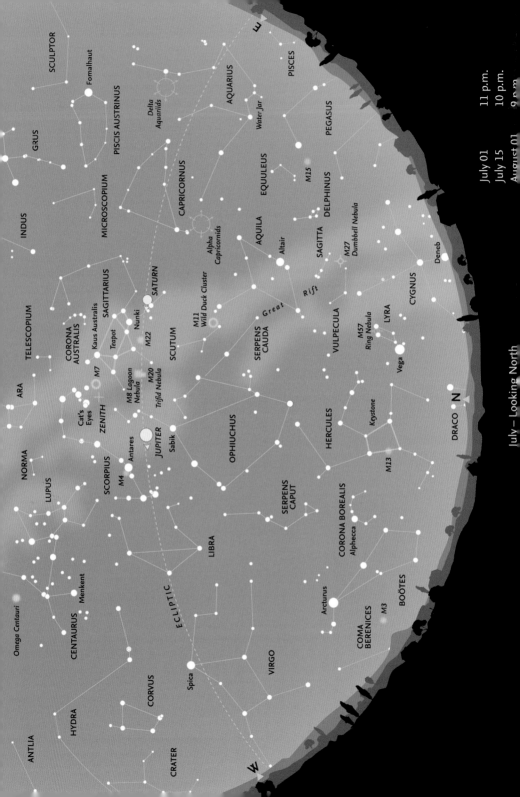

July – Looking North

July 01   11 p.m.
July 15   10 p.m.
August 01   9 p.m.

July – Looking North

The constellations of **Hercules** and **Lyra** are on either side of the meridian and both are clearly visible well above the horizon. To the east, **Deneb** (α Cygni) is skimming the horizon, but nearly all of the rest of the constellation is easily seen as is **Aquila** with **Altair** (α Aquilae). Between Cygnus and Aquila lies the small constellation of **Sagitta**, with **M27** (the Dumbbell Nebula, a planetary nebula). Even farther east, the whole extent of both the zodiacal constellations of **Aquarius** and **Capricornus** is visible. Above Aquila, farther along the **Great Rift** is the small constellation of **Scutum**, with **M11**, the Wild Duck Cluster. To its east is the tiny, but distinctive constellation of **Delphinus**. Still farther along the Great Rift lies the centre of the Milky Way Galaxy (in **Sagittarius**) and, near it, two emission nebulae: **M8** (the Lagoon Nebula) and **M20** (the Trifid Nebula). In the western sky, the constellations of **Boötes** and **Arcturus** (α Boötis) are beginning to approach the horizon, but **Corona Borealis** is still clearly seen. Even farther west, the whole of **Virgo** is visible, with **Libra** above it. The large constellation of **Ophiuchus** and the two halves of **Serpens** lie between Hercules and the zenith. **Scorpius** is draped around the actual zenith with Sagittarius to its east.

Part of the central Milky Way in the constellations of Norma and Scorpius, showing the dark clouds of obscuring dust (north is up).

The Moon's phases for July

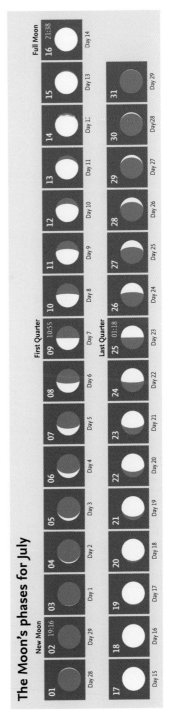

July – Moon and Planets

The Moon

New Moon occurs on July 2, when the Moon (and Sun) are in **Gemini**. That day there is a total solar eclipse, visible from the South Pacific and the southern tip of South America. On July 4, the Moon is very close to **Mars** in **Cancer**, but both bodies are lost in daylight. It passes **Regulus** in **Leo** on July 6, visible as the constellation sets in the west. On July 9, the Moon is close to **Spica** in **Virgo**, but before close approach, the objects are visible earlier in the night. On July 13 the Moon is close to **Antares** in **Scorpius** and then passes **Jupiter** in **Ophiuchus**. On July 16 it lies very close to **Saturn** in **Sagittarius**, but Full Moon occurs later in the day, so Saturn will be difficult to see. That day there is a partial lunar eclipse, visible from Africa and the Middle East. On July 28, the Moon is a waning crescent close to **Aldebaran**, in **Taurus**, visible only later as the objects rise in the east.

The planets

Mercury remains invisible in daylight and passes inferior conjunction (between Earth and the Sun) on July 21. **Venus** is also too close to the Sun to be detected. **Mars** remains close to the Sun in **Cancer**. **Jupiter** (mag. -2.6 to -2.4) is still retrograding slowly in **Ophiuchus** and **Saturn** (mag. 0.1) is doing the same in **Sagittarius**, reaching opposition on July 9. Its position at opposition (and that of Jupiter in June) is shown on the chart on page 18. **Uranus** is still in **Aries** at mag. 5.9 and **Neptune** in **Aquarius** at mag. 7.9.

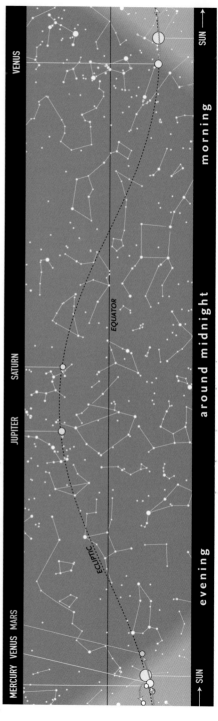

The path of the Sun and the planets along the ecliptic in July.

Calendar for July

1	21:45	Venus 1.6°N of Moon
2	19:16	New Moon
2	19:23	Total solar eclipse (S. Pacific, southern S. America)
3	18:24	Pollux 6.1°N of Moon
4	05:39	Mars 0.1°S of Moon
4	08:34	Mercury 3.2°S of Moon
4	22:11	Earth at aphelion (152,104,213 km = 1.01675 AU)
5	05:00	Moon at perigee (363,726 km)
6	02:42	Regulus 3.2°S of Moon
09	10:55	First Quarter
09	17:07	Saturn at opposition (mag. 0.1)
09	18:10	Spica 7.9°S of Moon
1–Aug.10		Alpha Capricornid meteor shower
3	07:19	Antares 8°S of Moon
3	19:43	Jupiter 2.3°S of Moon
3–Aug.26		Perseid meteor shower
6	07:15	Saturn 0.2°N of Moon
6	21:38	Full Moon
6	23:59	Partial lunar eclipse (Africa)
0	21:31	Moon at apogee (405,481 km)
1	12:34	Mercury at inferior conjunction
1–Aug.23		Delta Aquariid meteor shower
3	16:00 *	Venus 6.1°S of Pollux
5	01:18	Last Quarter
26–Aug.01		Alpha Capricornid shower maximum
8	01:16	Aldebaran 2.3°S of Moon
9–30		Delta Aquariid shower maximum
1	02:18	Mercury 4.5°S of Moon
1	04:29	Pollux 6.1°N of Moon
1	20:36	Venus 0.6°S of Moon

These objects are close together for an extended period around this time.

Evening 6:30 p.m.

July 6 • The Moon with Regulus and Algieba in the evening sky, in the northwest.

Evening 11 p.m.

July 13–16 • The waxing gibbous Moon passes Antares, Jupiter, Sabik, Nunki and Saturn, not far from the zenith.

Morning 5 a.m.

July 28 • The Moon is between Aldebaran and the Pleiades. Betelgeuse and Rigel are farther east.

Morning 6:30 a.m.

July 30–31 • The Moon with Alhena and Mercury. Mercury is rather faint (mag. 1.8) and hard to detect.

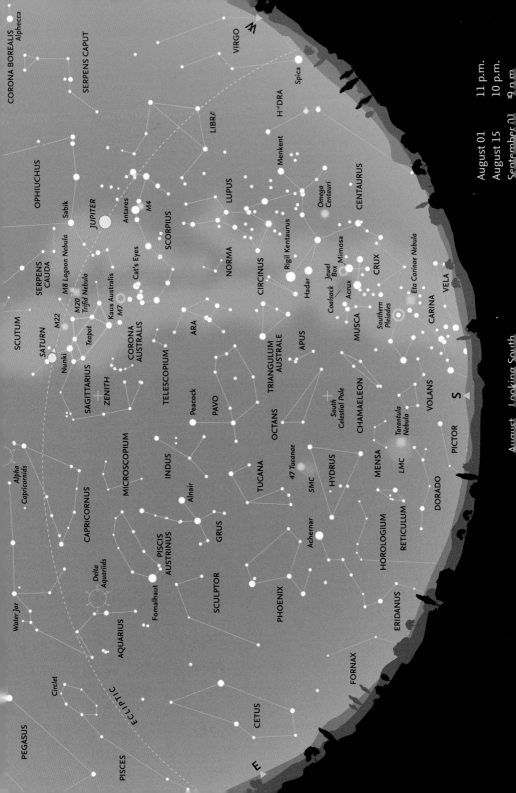

August — Looking South

August 01	11 p.m.
August 15	10 p.m.
September 01	9 p.m.

August – Looking South

Three inconspicuous constellations: *Volans*, *Chamaeleon* and *Octans* are on the meridian, with *Pavo* higher towards the zenith. Much of *Carina* is below the horizon, although the *Eta Carinae Nebula* and the *Southern Pleiades* are still visible. The *Large Magellanic Cloud* (LMC) and the faint constellation of *Mensa* are slightly higher in the sky. *Crux* is now lower, but the whole of *Centaurus* and *Lupus* remains visible. Much of *Virgo* has set in the west and *Libra* is following it down towards the horizon. *Scorpius* and *Sagittarius* are still visible high in the sky. *Achernar*, the *Large Magellanic Cloud* (SMC) and *Hydrus* are now well clear of the horizon, but below them are more small, inconspicuous constellations: *Dorado*, *Reticulum* and *Horlogium*. More of *Eridanus* is visible, together with parts of *Pictor* and *Fornax*. Much of *Cetus* has risen and the whole of the western arm of *Pisces* is now clearly seen. *Sculptor*, *Grus* and *Piscis Austrinus* lie half-way between the eastern horizon and the zenith, with faint *Microscopium* closer to the actual zenith.

Meteors

The *Piscis Austrinid* shower continues until about August 10, after maximum on July 27–28. The *Southern Delta Aquariids* reach maximum on July 29–30, but are unlikely to exhibit more than about 20 meteors per hour. There are several minor southern showers active during the month: the *Northern Delta Aquariids* (maximum August 13), the *Southern* and *Northern Iota Aquariids* (maxima August 4 and August 19, respectively), but in all cases the rates are very low, just single figures per hour.

The cross-shaped constellation of Grus. The brightest star, Alnair (α Gruis), in the centre of the image, is magnitude 1.8 (north is up).

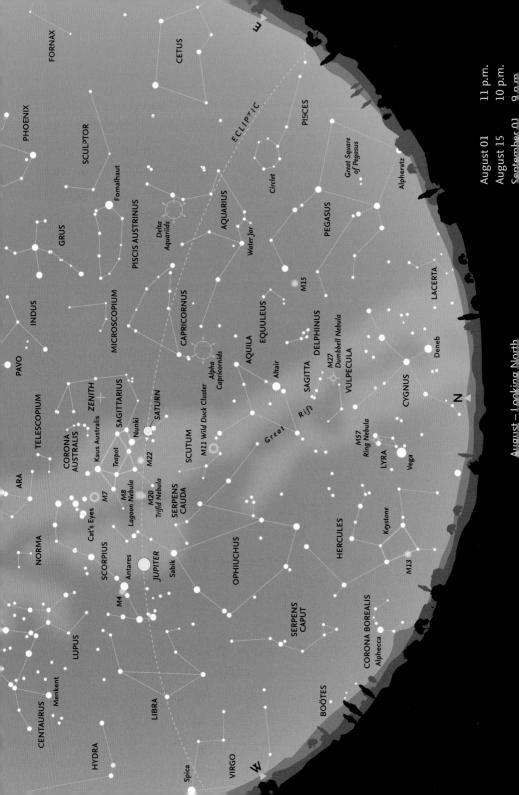

August – Looking North

August 01   11 p.m.
August 15   10 p.m.
September 01   9 p.m.

August – Looking North

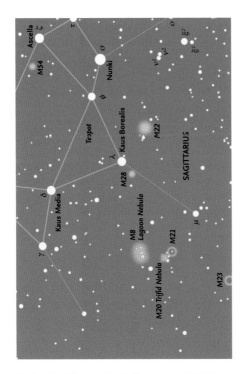

Cygnus, with brilliant Deneb (α Cygni), is now prominent just to the east of the meridian. The other two stars of the (northern) Summer Triangle, **Vega** in **Lyra** and **Altair** in **Aquila** are also unmistakeable in the sky. **Hercules,** however, is beginning to descend towards the northwestern horizon. Above it, the sprawling constellation of **Ophiuchus** is readily seen. The Great Square of **Pegasus** is now visible in the east, although **Alpheratz** (α Andromedae) is low on the horizon. The western side of **Pisces, Aquarius** and **Capricornus** are fully visible along the ecliptic. **Sagittarius,** with **M8** (the Lagoon Nebula) and **M20** (the Trifd Nebula) is at the zenith, with **Scorpius** to the west.

A finder chart for the gaseous nebulae M8 (the Lagoon Nebula) and M20 (the Trifid Nebula) and the globular cluster M22, all in Sagittarius. Clusters M21 & M23 (open) and M28 (globular) are faint. The chart shows all stars brighter than magnitude 7.5 (south is up).

The Moon's phases for August

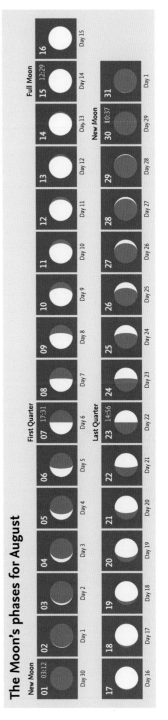

August – Moon and Planets

The Moon

New Moon occurs on August 1 in *Cancer*. A few hours later, it passes *Mars*, just inside *Leo* and the next day it is close to *Regulus*, but these events occur in daylight. On August 6, just before First Quarter, it passes *Spica* in *Virgo*, but the constellation is visible only as it sets in the west. On August 9, the Moon is close to both *Antares* in *Scorpius* and *Jupiter* (in *Ophiuchus*), visible just before they set. On August 12, the Moon occults *Saturn* in *Sagittarius*, with the event visible from New Zealand (particularly North Island) and eastern Australia (Sydney, Brisbane). Full Moon is on August 15, on the border of *Capricornus* and *Aquarius*. On August 30, at New Moon, the Sun, the Moon, *Mercury*, *Venus* and *Mars* are all clustered together in Leo.

The planets

Mercury is at greatest eastern elongation on August 9, but rapidly becomes close to the Sun. *Venus* is invisible near the Sun in daylight. It is at superior conjunction on August 14. *Mars* (in *Leo*) at mag. 1.8 is also too close to the Sun to be readily visible, but might be glimpsed early in the month as it sets in the west. *Jupiter* (mag. -2.4 to -2.2) is in *Ophiuchus*, reaches a stationary point on August 8 and then begins normal eastwards motion. *Saturn* (mag. 0.1 to 0.3) is still retrograding slowly in *Sagittarius*. An occultation is visible from New Zealand and eastern Australia. *Uranus* (mag. 5.9) and *Neptune* (mag. 7.9) remain in *Aries* and *Aquarius*, respectively.

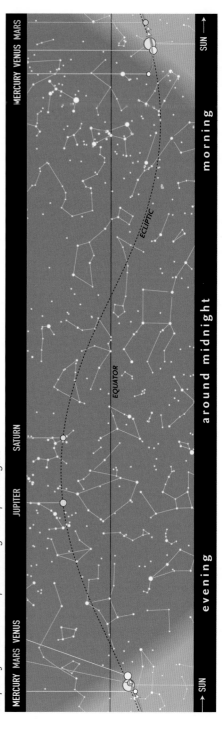

The path of the Sun and the planets along the ecliptic in August.

Calendar for August

01	03:12	New Moon
01	19:55	Mars 1.7°S of Moon
02	07:11	Moon at perigee (359,398 km)
02	11:41	Regulus 3.2°S of Moon
06	00:35	Spica 7.8°S of Moon
07	17:31	First Quarter
09	12:50	Antares 7.9°S of Moon
09	22:53	Jupiter 2.5°S of Moon
09	23:08	Mercury at greatest elongation (19.0°W, mag. –0.0)
11–12		Perseid shower maximum
12	09:53	Saturn 0.1°N of Moon (Occultation from NZ and E. Australia)
14	06:07	Venus at superior conjunction
15	12:29	Full Moon
17	10:49	Moon at apogee (406,244 km)
17	23:00 *	Mars 0.7°N of Regulus
21	04:00 *	Venus 1.0°N of Regulus
23	14:56	Last Quarter
24	09:54	Aldebaran 2.4°S of Moon
27	14:56	Pollux 6.1°N of Moon
28		Alpha Aurigid shower maximum
29	22:19	Regulus 3.2°S of Moon
30	01:07	Mercury 1.9°S of Moon
30	10:22	Mars 3.1°S of Moon
30	10:37	New Moon
30	15:53	Moon at perigee (357,176 km)
30	16:18	Venus 2.9°S of Moon

* These objects are close together for an extended period around this time.

Evening 9 p.m.

August 6 • The Moon Spica in the western sky. Arcturus is farther north.

After midnight 0:30 a.m.

August 9–11 • The Moon sets in the west, in the company of Antares, Jupiter and Sabik.

After midnight 2 a.m.

August 11–13 • The Moon with Nunki and Saturn. Kaus Australis and the Cat's Eyes are farther south.

Early morning 3 a.m.

August 23 • The Moon passes between Aldebaran and the Pleiades.

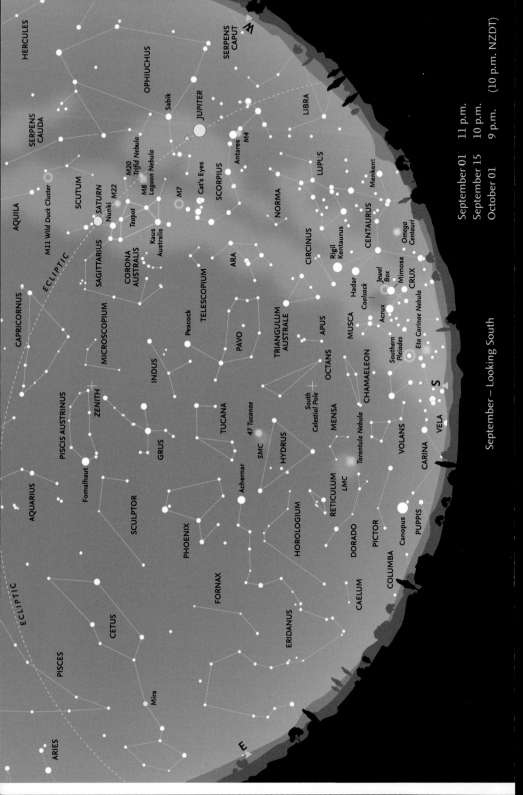

September 01   11 p.m.
September 15   10 p.m.
October 01   9 p.m.   (10 p.m. NZDT)

September – Looking South

September – Looking South

Crux is now very low, but **Canopus** (α Carinae) has now become visible once more. **Dorado** and the **Large Magellanic Cloud** (LMC) are higher and easier to see, as are the faint constellation of **Pictor, Caelum** and **Reticulum.** The **Small Magellanic Cloud** (SMC) and **47 Tucanae** are now nearly half-way between the horizon and the zenith. Although becoming low, the whole of **Centaurus** and **Lupus** remains visible in the southwest. **Scorpius** with reddish **Antares** is beginning to descend in the west, but **Sagittarius** is clearly seen high in the sky. The constellation of **Piscis Austrinus,** with **Fomalhaut** (α Piscis Austrini), is at the zenith. Below it are the constellations of **Grus** and **Pavo,** with **Achernar** (α Eridani) and almost the whole of the long constellation of **Eridanus.**

Meteors

There are no major meteor showers active in September, A few meteors may be seen from the **Alpha Aurigid** shower, active from late August, with possible double maxima on August 28 and September 15. There is one minor shower, the **Piscids,** active throughout September with a slight maximum on September 19, but with an overall rate of no more than 3–5 meteors per hour. However, September shows a considerable increase in the number of sporadic meteors.

The 'Teapot' of Sagittarius is in the upper half of the image and, just below the centre, the small curl of stars that is Corona Australis.

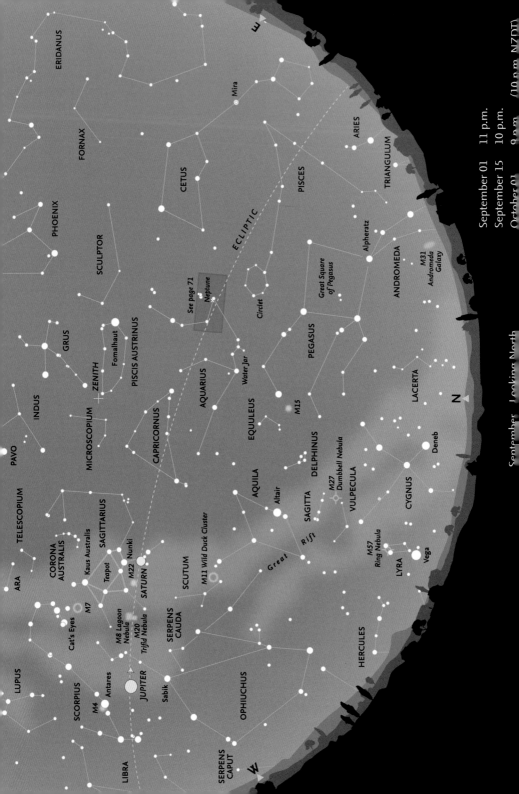

E

Mira

ERIDANUS

FORNAX

CETUS

ARIES

TRIANGULUM

PHOENIX

SCULPTOR

PISCES

ECLIPTIC

Neptune
See page 71

ANDROMEDA

Alpheratz

Great Square
of Pegasus

M31
Andromeda
Galaxy

GRUS

Circlet

PISCIS AUSTRINUS

Fomalhaut

ZENITH

Water Jar

PEGASUS

LACERTA

AQUARIUS

INDUS

MICROSCOPIUM

CAPRICORNUS

EQUULEUS

M15

PAVO

N

DELPHINUS

Deneb

AQUILA

TELESCOPIUM

ARA

CORONA
AUSTRALIS

SAGITTARIUS

Altair

SAGITTA

M27
Dumbbell Nebula

VULPECULA

CYGNUS

Kaus Australis

Teapot

M22 Nunki

SATURN

SCUTUM

Great Rift

M57
Ring Nebula

LYRA

Vega

M7

Cat's Eyes

M8 Lagoon
Nebula

M20
Trifid Nebula

SERPENS
CAUDA

M11 Wild Duck Cluster

HERCULES

LUPUS

M4

Antares

SCORPIUS

JUPITER

Sabik

OPHIUCHUS

LIBRA

SERPENS
CAPUT

W

September 01   11 p.m.
September 15   10 p.m.
October 01   9 p.m.   (10 p.m. NZDT)

September Looking North

September – Looking North

The Great Square of *Pegasus* is nearing the meridian from the east and, on the west, the three bright stars of *Deneb* (α Cygni), *Altair* (α Aquilae) and *Vega* (α Lyrae) are still clearly seen, although Vega is low on the horizon, as is *M31* in *Andromeda*. In the east, the whole of *Cetus* has become visible and the zodiacal constellation of *Pisces* is also clear of the horizon. *Delphinus* is well-placed, as are the fainter constellations of *Sagitta* and *Scutum* along the Milky Way. Giant *Ophiuchus* is beginning to descend towards the western horizon and much of *Libra* has disappeared. The three zodiacal constellations of *Pisces, Aquarius* and *Capricornus* are readily visible. Somewhat higher, *Pisces Austrinus* with *Fomalhaut* (α Pisces Austrini) is at the zenith. *Scorpius* and *Sagittarius* are now on the western side of the sky.

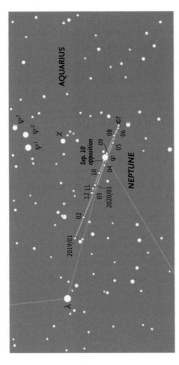

The path of Neptune in 2019. Neptune comes to opposition on September 10. All stars brighter than magnitude 8.5 are shown (south is up).

The Moon's phases for September

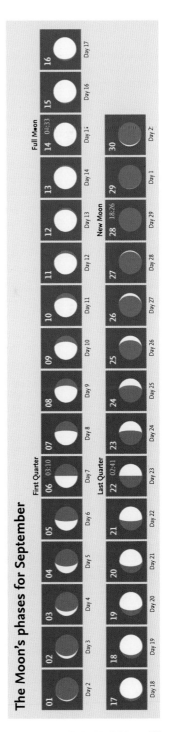

September – Moon and Planets

The Moon

On September 5, one day before First Quarter, the Moon is close to *Antares* and, the next day, near *Jupiter* in *Ophiuchus*. On September 8, 9 days old, it occults *Saturn* in *Sagittarius*. The event is visible from a wide area of northern and western Australia, including Darwin and Perth. Full Moon (in *Pisces*) is on September 14. By September 20, as waning gibbous, the Moon is close to *Aldebaran* in *Taurus*. On September 26, the Moon is close to *Regulus* in *Leo*, visible in the early morning before sunrise. New Moon is on September 28 when the Moon (and the Sun) are in *Virgo*.

The planets

Mercury and *Venus* are too close to the Sun and too low to be visible. *Mars* is also lost in daylight. *Jupiter* (mag. -2.2 to -2.0) is moving eastwards slowly in *Ophiuchus*. *Saturn* (mag. 0.3 to 0.5) is also moving eastwards slowly in *Sagittarius*. *Uranus* (mag. 5.9) is in *Aries*. *Neptune* (in *Aquarius*) comes to opposition on September 10 at mag. 7.8 (on page 71 there is a finder chart showing the path of Neptune in 2019).

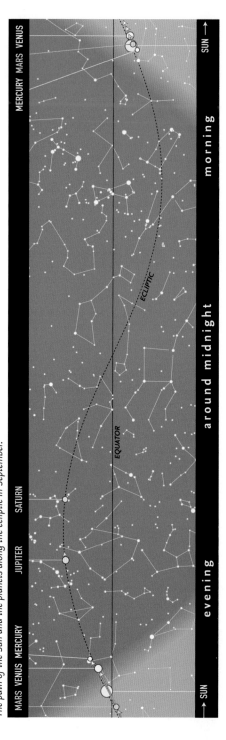

The path of the Sun and the planets along the ecliptic in September.

MARS VENUS MERCURY   JUPITER   SATURN

MERCURY MARS VENUS

SUN ←

← SUN

evening   around midnight   morning

SUN →

ECLIPTIC

EQUATOR

Calendar for September

2	09:13	Spica 7.7°S of Moon
2	10:42	Mars in conjunction with Sun
4	01:40	Mercury at superior conjunction
5	19:06	Antares 7.8°S of Moon
6	03:10	First Quarter
6	06:52	Jupiter 2.3°S of Moon
8	13:42	Saturn 0.1°N of Moon
		(Occultation from N. & W. Australia)
0	07:24	Neptune at opposition (mag. 7.8)
3	13:32	Moon at apogee (406,377 km)
4	04:33	Full Moon
5		Alpha Aurigid shower second maximum
0	16:45	Aldebaran 2.7°S of Moon
2	02:41	Last Quarter
3	07:50	Autumnal equinox
3–Nov.20		Southern Taurids meteor shower
3–Nov.27		Orionid meteor shower
4	00:01	Pollux 3.3°N of Moon
6	08:54	Regulus 3.3°S of Moon
8	01:19	Mars 4.1°S of Moon
8	02:24	Moon at perigee (357,802 km)
8	18:26	New Moon
9	12:46	Mars 4.4°S of Moon
9	19:44	Spica 7.6°S of Moon
9	-	Daylight Saving Time begins (New Zealand)
9	22:01	Mercury 6.2°S of Moon

Evening 11 p.m.

September 5–6 • The Moon with Antares, Jupiter and Sabik, before it sets in the southwest.

Occultation of Saturn

Perth
14:01:04 to
15:02:05 UT

Darwin
14:36:12 to
15:49:35 UT

September 8 • The occultation of Saturn, as seen from Perth (top) and Darwin (bottom). Time is given in UT.

Morning 4 a.m.

September 23–25 • The Moon passes Alhena and the twin stars Castor and Pollux low in the northeast.

Morning 5:15 a.m.

September 26–27 • The Moon passes between Regulus and Algieba, which is probably lost in dawn.

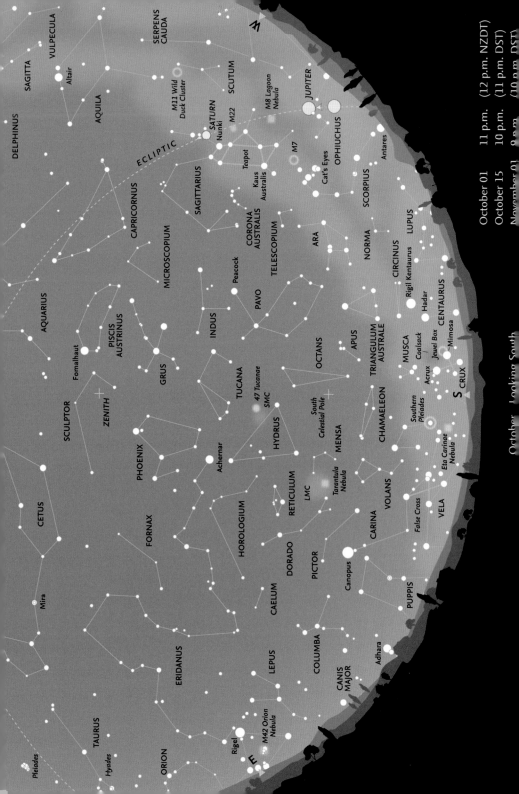

October 01   11 p.m.   (12 p.m. NZDT)
October 15   10 p.m.   (11 p.m. DST)
November 01   9 p.m.   (10 p.m. DST)

October, Looking South

October – Looking South

Crux is now extremely low, only just visible above the horizon. The **False Cross** has reappeared, also low, farther towards the east on the opposite side of the meridian. **Canopus** (α Carinae) is now much higher as is the **Large Magellanic Cloud** (LMC). The **Small Magellanic Cloud** (SMC) and **47 Tucanae** are on the southern meridian, half-way to the zenith, as is **Achernar** (α Eridani). (The whole of the long constellation of **Eridanus** is now visible together with **Rigel** in **Orion**.) Still higher are **Phoenix**, **Grus** and **Piscis Austrinus**. **Pavo** has begun to descend in the southwest. **Ophiuchus** has now slipped below the horizon as has much of **Scorpius**, only the 'tail' of which remains visible. **Sagittarius** is getting lower, but remains visible, as do the zodiacal constellations of **Capricornus** and **Aquarius.**

Meteors

The **Orionids** are the major, fairly reliable meteor shower active in October. Like the May **Eta Aquariid** shower, the Orionids are associated with Comet 1P/Halley. During this second pass through the stream of particles from the comet, slightly fewer meteors are seen than in May. In both showers the meteors are very fast, and many leave persistent trains. Although the Orionid maximum is quoted as October 21–22, in fact there is a very broad maximum, lasting about a week from October 20 to 27, with hourly rates around 25. Occasionally rates are higher (50–70 per hour). In 2019, the broad maximum extends from the day before Last Quarter to a waning crescent, so moonlight should not cause too much interference.

The faint shower of the **Southern Taurids** (often with bright fireballs) peaks on October 28–29. The Southern Taurid maximum occurs around New Moon, so conditions are generally favourable. Towards the end of the month (around October 19), another shower (the **Northern**

The Small Magellanic Cloud, one of the satellite galaxies to the Milky Way. Near the right edge of this image is 47 Tucanae (NGC 104), which is the second brightest globular cluster, after Omega Centauri (see page 51). North is up.

Taurids) begins to show activity, which peaks early in November. The parent comet for both Taurid showers is Comet 2P/Encke.

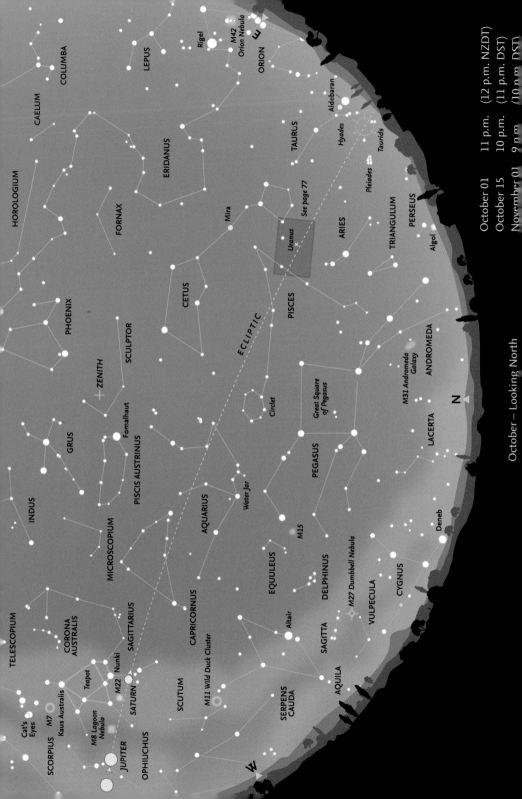

October – Looking North

October – Looking North

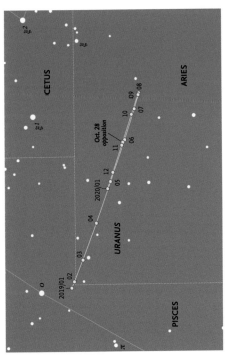

The Great Square of *Pegasus* now dominates the sky to the north and the whole of *Andromeda* with the *Andromeda Galaxy* (M31) is now clear of the horizon. The two chains of stars forming *Pisces* frame the Great Square and, farther along the ecliptic, the constellations of *Aquarius* and *Capricornus* are fully visible. Farther east, all of *Cetus* is visible and, low down on the horizon, *Aldebaran* in *Taurus* is beginning to rise. Due east *Orion* is becoming visible, with blue-white *Rigel* and the beginning of the long, winding constellation of *Eridanus* that wends its way to *Achernar* (α Eridani), far to the south. West of the meridian, *Lyra*, with *Vega* has disappeared; much of *Cygnus* is invisible and *Deneb* is brushing the horizon. Only *Aquila* and *Altair* (α Aquilae) remain clearly visible. *Vulpecula*, with the planetary nebula *M27* is still visible as is *Sagitta* and, above them, the distinctive constellation of *Delphinus* and the very faint, inconspicuous constellation of *Equuleus*.

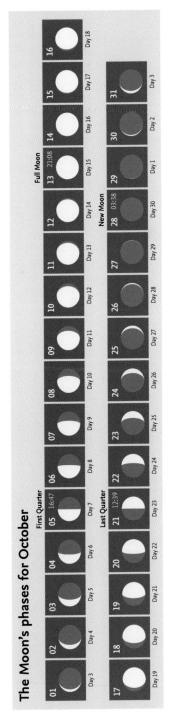

The path of Uranus in 2019. Uranus comes to opposition on October 28. All stars brighter than magnitude 7.5 are shown (south is up).

The Moon's phases for October

October – Moon and Planets

The Moon

The Moon is near **Antares** on October 3, but is visible only early just before setting. Later that day it is close to **Jupiter** and both bodies may be glimpsed just before they set in the west. On October 5, the Moon passes very close to **Saturn**. (There is an occultation visible from southern Africa.) Full Moon is on October 13. On October 17, the waning gibbous Moon is close to **Aldebaran** in **Taurus** and on October 23 it is near **Regulus** in **Leo**, but the constellation rises only later the next morning. New Moon occurs on October 28.

The planets

Mercury comes to greatest eastern elongation on October 20, but is invisible in daylight in **Libra**. **Venus** remains close to the Sun, also in Libra and not visible. **Mars** (in **Virgo**) is similarly too close to the Sun to be seen. **Jupiter** (mag. -2.0 to -1.9) is moving slowly eastwards in **Ophiuchus** and is visible in the early evening before it sets, as is **Saturn** in **Sagittarius** at mag. 0.5. **Uranus** remains in **Aries**, and comes to opposition on October 28 at mag. 5.7 (on page 77 there is a finder chart showing the path of Uranus in 2019). **Neptune** is in **Aquarius** at mag. 7.9. Both constellations are visible for a large part of the night.

The path of the Sun and the planets along the ecliptic in October.

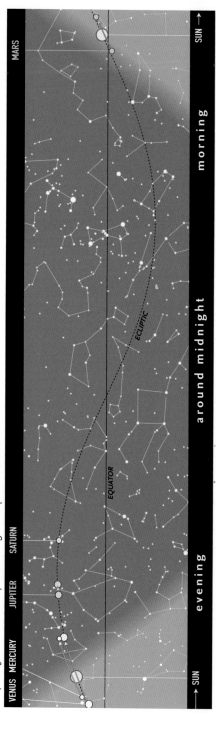

Calendar for October

03	01:00 *	Venus 3.1°N of Spica
03	03:18	Antares 7.5°S of Moon
03	20:23	Jupiter 1.9°S of Moon
05	16:47	First Quarter
05	20:36	Saturn 0.3°N of Moon
		(Occultation from S. Africa)
06		Daylight Saving Time begins
		(Australia)
10	18:29	Moon at apogee (405,898 km)
13	21:08	Full Moon
17	22:22	Aldebaran 2.9°S of Moon
19–Dec.10		Northern Taurid meteor shower
20	04:02	Mercury at greatest elongation
		(24.6°E, mag. −0.1)
21	06:49	Pollux 5.6°N of Moon
21	12:39	Last Quarter
21–22		Orionid shower maximum
23	17:37	Regulus 3.5°S of Moon
26	10:39	Moon at perigee (363,101 km)
26	16:52	Mars 4.5°S of Moon
27	06:30	Spica 7.6°S of Moon
28	03:38	New Moon
28	08:15	Uranus at opposition (mag. 5.7)
28–29		Southern Taurid shower maximum
29	14:55	Mercury 6.7°S of Moon
29	13:32	Venus 3.9°S of Moon
30	13:14	Antares 7.3°S of Moon
31	14:22	Jupiter 1.3°S of Moon

* These objects are close together for an extended period around this time.

Occultation of Saturn

Durban
21:46:29 to
22:21:58 UT

Pretoria
21:43:06 to
22:31:40 UT

Cape Town
21:49:10 *

* The Moon sets before the occultation ends

October 5 • The occultation of Saturn, as seen from three locations in South Africa. Time is given in UT.

Evening 10 p.m. (DST)

Antares • Jupiter • 4
3
2
10°
WSW • W

October 2–4 • The waxing crescent Moon passes Antares, Sabik and Jupiter in the evening sky.

Evening 11:30 p.m. (DST)

Pleiades • Moon • Aldebaran
10°
NE • ENE

October 17 • The Moon is between Aldebaran and the Pleiades.

After midnight 0:30 a.m. (DST)

Nunki • Saturn • Moon
10°
WSW • W

October 6 • The Moon with Saturn and Nunki.

Evening 8 p.m. (DST)

Antares • Sabik • 30
Mercury • Venus • 29
10°
WSW • W

October 29–30 • The Moon with Mercury and Venus after sunset.

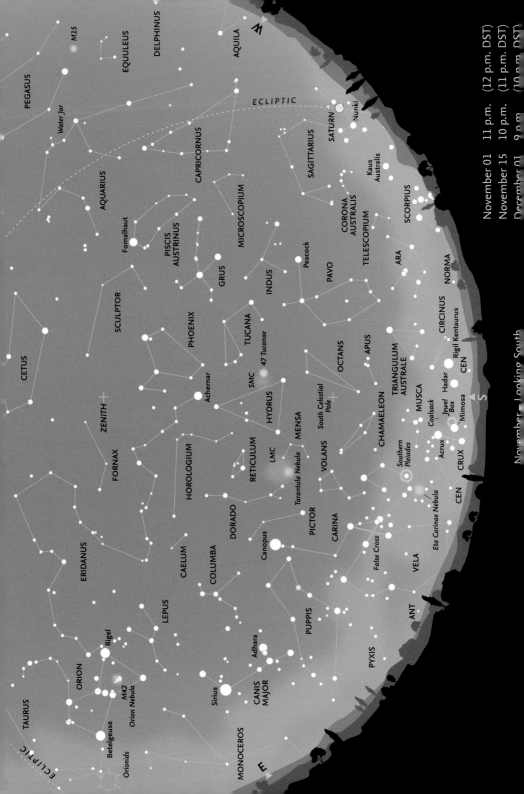

November 01   11 p.m.   (12 p.m. DST)
November 15   10 p.m.   (11 p.m. DST)
December 01   9 p.m.   (10 p.m. DST)

November – Looking South

November – Looking South

Crux and the two brightest stars of **Centaurus**, **Rigil Kentaurus** (α Centauri) and **Hadar** (β Centauri), are extremely low on the southern horizon. The **False Cross** on the **Carina/Vela** border is now higher, and the constellation of **Puppis** as well as **Canopus** (α Carinae) and both the **Large Magellanic Cloud** (LMC) and the **Small Magellanic Cloud** (SMC) are clearly visible. **Achernar** (α Eridani) is half-way between the South Celestial Pole and the zenith. The whole of **Eridanus**, which starts near **Rigel** in **Orion**, is now clearly seen as it winds its way to Achernar. **Pavo** is becoming lower in the southwest, and in the west most of **Sagittarius** is below the horizon, with **Capricornus** descending behind it. **Corona Australis** is still just visible. In the west, **Canis Major** is now clearly seen, together with the small constellations of **Columba** and **Lepus** above it.

Meteors

Two meteor showers begin in October but continue into November. The **Orionids** (see page 75), one of the streams associated with Comet 1/P Halley, continue until at least November 27. Because of the location of the radiant, the **Leonid** shower is best seen from the northern hemisphere, but southern observers may see some rising from the horizon. There is a short period of activity (November 5–30), with maximum on November 17–18. This shower is associated with Comet 55P/Tempel-Tuttle and has shown extraordinary activity on various occasions with many thousands of meteors per hour. The rate in 2019 is likely to be about 15 per hour. These meteors are the fastest shower meteors recorded (about 70 km per second) and often leave persistent trains. The shower is very rich in faint meteors.

There is a minor southern meteor shower that begins activity in late November (nominally November 28). This is the **Phoenicids**, but little is known of the shower, partly because the parent comet is believed to be the disintegrated comet D/1819 W1 (Blanpain). With no accurate

knowledge of the location of the remnants of the comet, predicting the possible rate becomes little more than guesswork, but the rate is variable and may rapidly increase (as might be expected), if the orbit is nearby. Bright meteors tend to be quite frequent and the meteors are fairly slow. The radiant is located within Phoenix, not far from the border with **Eridanus** and **Achernar** (α Eridani).

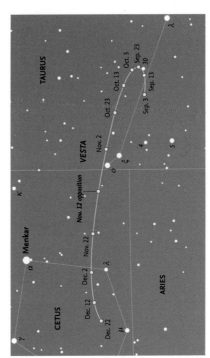

A finder chart for minor planet Vesta (4) which is at opposition (mag. 6.5) on November 12. Background stars are shown down to magnitude 7.5 (south is up).

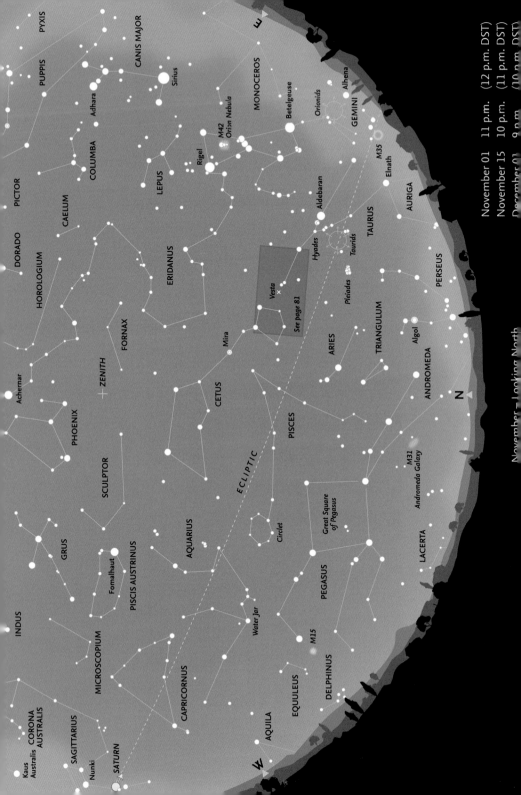

November – Looking North

November 01   11 p.m.   (12 p.m. DST)
November 15   10 p.m.   (11 p.m. DST)
December 01   9 p.m.   (10 p.m. DST)

November – Looking North

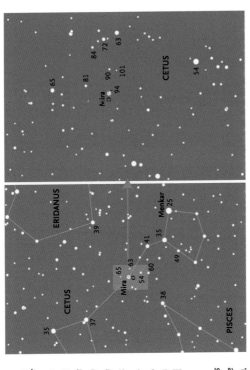

Andromeda is now due north, and the **Andromeda Galaxy** (M31) has risen sufficiently to be clearly seen. The constellation of **Triangulum** lies between Andromeda and the zodiacal constellation of **Aries**. Much of **Perseus** (including the variable star, **Algol**) is now above the horizon. The whole of **Pegasus**, with the **Great Square**, is clearly seen and, above it the two lines of stars forming **Pisces**. Higher still is the constellation of **Cetus** with the famous variable star, **Mira**. The whole of **Taurus** with **Aldebaran** (α Tauri), the **Pleiades** and the **Hyades** is visible in the southeast. **Orion** has fully risen in the east, and the whole of **Eridanus** is visible as it winds its long way to **Achernar** (α Eridani), south of the zenith. In the west, the zodiacal constellations of **Aquarius** and **Capricornus** are clearly seen, with **Piscis Austrinus** and bright **Fomalhaut** (α Piscis Austrini) higher in the sky, with the faint constellation of **Sculptor** lying between it and the zenith.

Finder and comparison charts for Mira (o Ceti). The chart on the left shows all stars brighter than magnitude 6.5. The chart on the right shows stars down to magnitude 10.0. The comparison star magnitudes are shown without the decimal point (south is up).

The Moon's phases for November

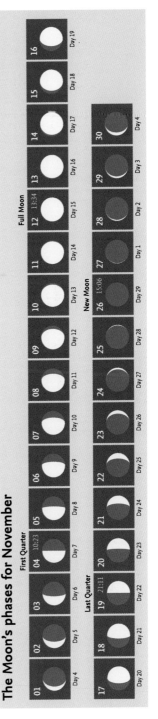

November – Moon and Planets

The Moon

On November 2 the Moon (a waxing crescent, two days before First Quarter) is very close to **Saturn** in **Sagittarius**. (There is an occultation, visible from New Zealand and the southern tip of Tasmania.) Full Moon is on November 12, when the Moon is on the border of **Aries** with **Taurus**. Two days later, on November 14, the Moon is north of **Aldebaran**. On November 19, at Last Quarter, it is near **Regulus** in **Leo**. On November 23, a waning crescent, it passes **Spica** in **Virgo** and, a day later, is close to **Mars**. The three bodies are visible in the early-morning sky. New Moon is on November 26, when it is in the small section of **Scorpius** between **Libra** and **Ophiuchus**. Two days later it is close to **Jupiter** in the morning sky, and on November 29 it is again close to **Saturn**.

The planets

Mercury is initially close to the Sun, passing inferior conjunction on November 11, but rapidly moves to greatest western elongation on November 28, when it may be glimpsed in the morning sky. **Venus** (mag. -3.8 to -3.9) is very low in the evening sky. **Mars** (mag. 1.8–1.7) is in **Libra**, visible in the early morning. **Jupiter** (mag. -1.9 to -1.8), initially in **Ophiuchus**, moves into **Sagittarius** and is visible in the southwest just before it sets. **Saturn** (mag. 0.5–0.6) is also in **Sagittarius**. **Uranus** is mag. 5.7 in **Aries** and **Neptune** (mag .7.9) is in **Aquarius**. The minor planet (4) **Vesta** comes to opposition in **Cetus** on November 12. There is a finder chart on page 81.

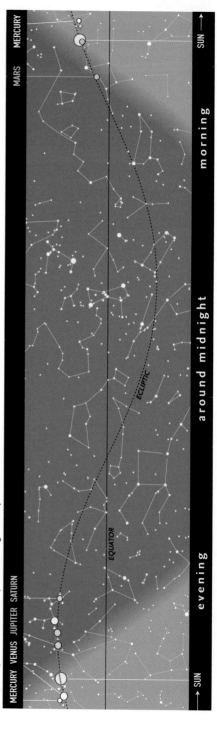

The path of the Sun and the planets along the ecliptic in November.

Calendar for November

Date	Time	Event
02	07:21	Saturn 0.6°N of Moon
		Occultation from New Zealand
		and Tasmania
04	10:23	First Quarter
07	08:36	Moon at apogee (405,058 km)
08	15:00 *	Mars 3.0°N of Spica
09	11:00 *	Venus 4.0°N of Antares
10–11		Northern Taurids shower maximum
11	15:22	Mercury at inferior conjunction
12	08:56	Vesta at opposition (mag. 6.5)
12	13:34	Full Moon
14	04:23	Aldebaran 3.0°S of Moon
17	12:10	Pollux 5.4°N of Moon
17–18		Leonids shower maximum
19	21:11	Last Quarter
19	23:51	Regulus 3.7°S of Moon
23	07:41	Moon at perigee (366,716 km)
23	15:32	Spica 7.7°S of Moon
24	09:02	Mars 4.3°S of Moon
24	14:00 *	Venus 1.4°S of Jupiter
25	02:50	Mercury 1.9°S of Moon
26	15:06	New Moon
26	23:29	Antares 7.2°S of Moon
28	10:29	Mercury at greatest elongation
		(20.1°W, mag. -0.6)
28	10:49	Jupiter 0.7°S of Moon
28	18:49	Venus 1.9°S of Moon
28–Dec.09		Phoenicid meteor shower
29	21:03	Saturn 0.9°N of Moon

* These objects are close together for an extended period around this time.

Evening 10 p.m. (DST)

Kaus Australis •   Nunki •   Nov 2   Saturn •

Jupiter   Nov 1

Oct 31

Cat's Eyes

WSW   W

10°

October 31 – November 2 • The waxing crescent Moon passes Jupiter, Nunki and Saturn in the west.

Morning 5:15 a.m. (DST)

Spica •

24

Mars •

25   Mercury

E   ESE

10°

November 24–25 • The waning crescent Moon with Spica, Mars and Mercury shortly before sunrise.

Morning 5:30 a.m. (DST)

Porrima •

Mars

Spica

E   ESE

10°

November 9 • Spica (mag. 1.0) and Mars (mag. 1.8) close together before sunrise. Porrima (γ Vir) is nearby.

Evening 8:30 p.m. (DST)

30   Saturn •

Kaus Australis •   Nunki •

Venus   29

28

Jupiter

Cat's Eyes

WSW   W

10°

November 28–30 • After sunset the narrow crescent Moon passes Jupiter, Venus, Nunki and Saturn.

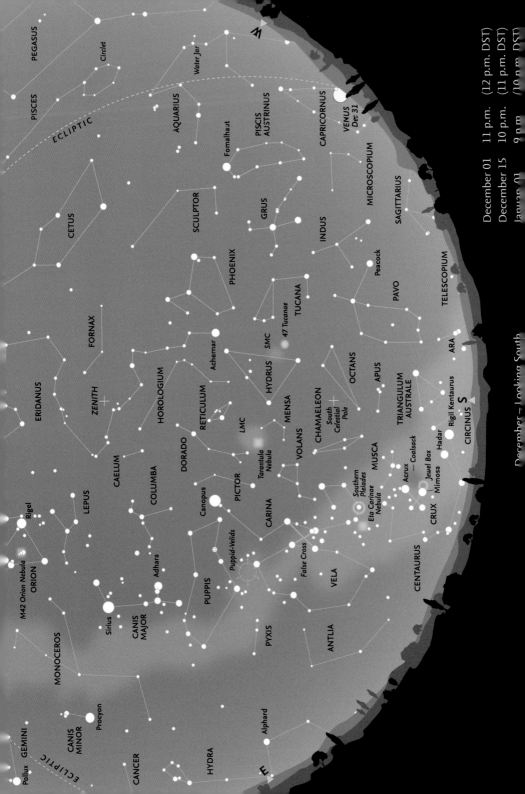

December – Looking South

December 01   11 p.m.   (12 p.m. DST)
December 15   10 p.m.   (11 p.m. DST)
January 01   9 p.m.   (10 p.m. DST)

PEGASUS
Circlet
PISCES
Water Jar
M
AQUARIUS
ECLIPTIC
PISCIS
AUSTRINUS
CAPRICORNUS
VENUS
Dec 31
Fomalhaut
GRUS
MICROSCOPIUM
CETUS
SCULPTOR
PHOENIX
INDUS
SAGITTARIUS
FORNAX
Peacock
PAVO
TELESCOPIUM
ERIDANUS
47 Tucanae
TUCANA
SMC
Achernar
ARA
ZENITH
HOROLOGIUM
RETICULUM
HYDRUS
OCTANS
APUS
CIRCINUS
S
CAELUM
DORADO
LMC
MENSA
CHAMAELEON
South
Celestial
Pole
TRIANGULUM
AUSTRALE
Rigil Kentaurus
LEPUS
COLUMBA
Tarantula
Nebula
VOLANS
MUSCA
Hadar
Rigel
PICTOR
Coalsack
Acrux
Jewel Box
ORION
M42 Orion Nebula
Canopus
CARINA
Southern
Pleiades
Eta Carinae
Nebula
CRUX
Mimosa
Adhara
Puppis-Velids
False Cross
CENTAURUS
Sirius
CANIS
MAJOR
PUPPIS
VELA
MONOCEROS
ANTLIA
PYXIS
Procyon
CANIS
MINOR
Alphard
GEMINI
Pollux
ECLIPTIC
CANCER
HYDRA
E

December – Looking South

Crux and the two brightest stars in **Centaurus**, **Hadar** and **Rigil Kentaurus**, are now higher above the horizon. **The Eta Carina Nebula** and the **Southern Pleiades** are now conveniently placed for observation. Above them, the **False Cross** is clearly seen, with the whole of **Vela** and below it the inconspicuous constellation of **Antlia**. **Carina** with **Canopus** (α Carinae) and **Puppis** are roughly halfway between the horizon and the zenith. **Sirius** and **Canis Major** are high in the east. In the west, **Achernar** (α Eridani) and **Phoenix** are about the same altitude as Canopus. The faint constellations of **Pictor**, **Dorado**, **Reticulum**, and **Horologium** lie between them. **Pavo** with Peacock (α Pavonis) is becoming low, as are the constellations of **Indus**, **Grus** and **Piscis Austrinus**. Higher still are the inconspicuous constellations of **Sculptor** and, near the zenith, **Fornax**. **Capricornus** is largely invisible, but most of **Aquarius** may still be seen.

Meteors

The **Phoenicid** shower continues into December, reaching its weak maximum on December 2. The **Puppid Velid** shower's radiant is on the border between the two constellations. The shower begins on December 1, lasting until December 15, with maximum on December 7. It is a weak shower with a maximum hourly rate of about 10 meteors, but bright meteors are often seen. One of the most dependable showers of the year is the **Geminids**, active from December 4 to 16, with maximum in 2019 on December 13–14. The rate is ofter more than 60–70 per hour and may rise even higher.

The Large Magellanic Cloud seen over the European Southern Observatory at Paranal in Chile. Brilliant Canopus (α Carinae), the brightest star in the southern hemisphere, is visible through the low cloud to the right.

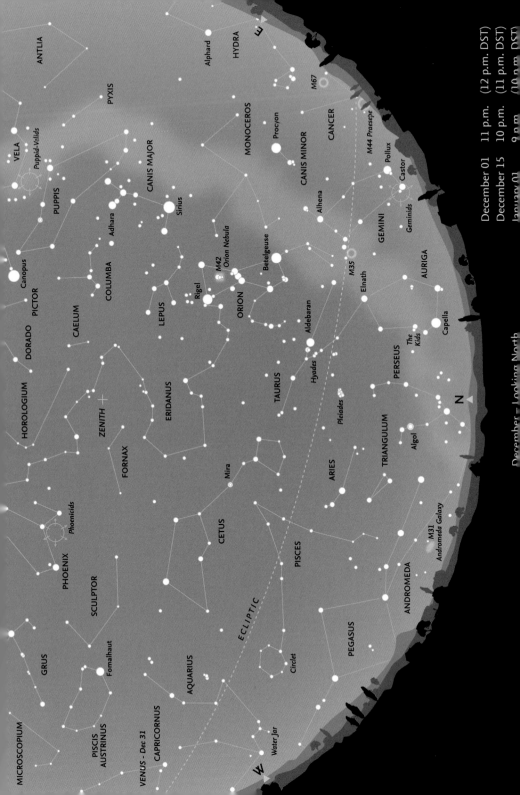

December – Looking North

December 01   11 p.m.   (12 p.m. DST)
December 15   10 p.m.   (11 p.m. DST)
January 01   9 p.m.   (10 p.m. DST)

December – Looking North

Most of **Perseus** may be seen due north with, above it, the *Pleiades* cluster. Farther west, **Andromeda** is very low and the southern stars of **Pegasus** have been lost below the horizon. Above Pegasus lies the zodiacal constellation of **Pisces** and, still higher, **Cetus** and the faint constellatons of **Sculptor** and **Fornax**. The famous variable of **Mira** in Cetus (see charts on page 83) is ideally placed for observation. Towards the east the whole of the constellations of both **Auriga** and **Gemini** is visible, although **Capella** (α Aurigae) and **Castor** and **Pollux** (α and β Gemini) are low on the horizon. **Taurus, Orion** and **Canis Minor** are readily visible, together with the faint constellation of **Monoceros.** **Eridanus** wanders from its start near **Rigel** (β Orionis) towards **Achernar** (α Eridani), beyond the zenith.

The constellation of Taurus contains two contrasting open clusters: the compact Pleiades, with its striking blue-white stars, and the more scattered, 'V'-shaped Hyades, which are much closer to us. Orange Aldebaran (α Tauri) is not related to the Hyades, but lies between it and the Earth (south is up).

The Moon's phases for December

Last Quarter
First Quarter
Full Moon
New Moon

01	02	03	04 06:58	05	06	07	08
Day 5	Day 6	Day 7	Day 8	Day 9	Day 10	Day 11	Day 12
09	10	11	12 05:12	13	14	15	16
Day 13	Day 14	Day 15	Day 16	Day 17	Day 18	Day 19	Day 20
17	18	19 04:57	20	21	22	23	24
Day 21	Day 22	Day 23	Day 24	Day 25	Day 26	Day 27	Day 28
25	26 05:13	27	28	29	30	31	
Day 29	Day 30	Day 1	Day 2	Day 3	Day 4	Day 5	

December – Moon and Planets

The Moon

The Moon is close to **Aldebaran** in **Taurus** on December 11, but Full Moon occurs next day, so the star is overpowered by moonlight. On December 17, as waning gibbous, two days before Last Quarter, it is near **Regulus** in **Leo**, and on December 20, one day after Last Quarter, it is fairly close to **Spica** in **Virgo**. On December 23, as a waning crescent, it is close to **Mars** in **Libra**. At New Moon on December 26 there is an annular eclipse of the Sun, visible from Arabia, the Indian Ocean and Indonesia.

The planets

Mercury is rapidly approaching the Sun and is not visible. **Venus** begins the month low in the southwestern evening sky at mag. -3.9, and rapidly moves east into **Capricornus**, becoming more easily seen and brightening slightly. **Mars** (mag. 1.7) begins the month just inside **Virgo** and moves east into **Libra**. **Jupiter** is close to the **Sun** in **Sagittarius**, and **Saturn** is also in that constellation. **Uranus** is still just inside **Aries** near the border with **Pisces**, and **Neptune** remains in **Aquarius** where it has been throughout the year.

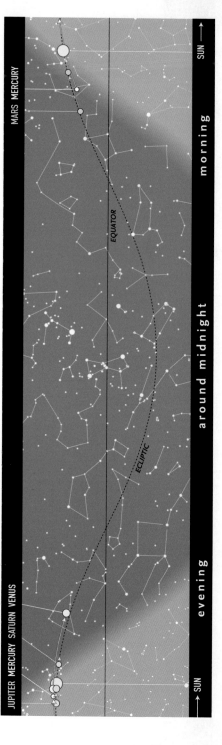

The path of the Sun and the planets along the ecliptic in December.

Calendar for December

01–15		Puppid Velid meteor shower
02		Phoenicid shower maximum
04	06:58	First Quarter
04–16		Geminid meteor shower
05	04:08	Moon at apogee (404,446 km)
07		Puppid Velid shower maximum
11	12:10	Aldebaran 3.0°S of Moon
12	05:12	Full Moon
13–14		Geminid shower maximum
14	18:19	Pollux 5.3°N of Moon
17	05:08	Regulus 3.8°S of Moon
18	20:25	Moon at perigee (370,265 km)
19	04:57	Last Quarter
20	22:03	Spica 7.8°S of Moon
22	04:19	Southern summer solstice
23	01:49	Mars 3.5°S of Moon
24	08:12	Antares 7.7°S of Moon
25	11:08	Mercury 1.9°S of Moon
26	05:13	New Moon
26	07:30	Jupiter 0.2°S of Moon
26	05:17	Annular solar eclipse (Arabia, Indian Ocean, Indonesia)
27	11:47	Saturn 1.2°N of Moon
27	18:26	Jupiter in conjunction with Sun
29	01:31	Venus 1.0°N of Moon

Evening 9 p.m. (DST)

December 10–11 • The Moon passes the Pleiades and Aldebaran. Betelgeuse and Rigel are farther east.

Morning 5 a.m. (DST)

December 23–24 • The Moon with Mars (mag. 1.6) and Antares (mag. 1.1).

After midnight 2 a.m. (DST)

December 17–18 • The Moon passes between Regulus and Algieba.

Evening 9 p.m. (DST)

December 28–29 • Shortly after sunset the narrow crescent Moon is in the west, in the company of Venus.

Glossary and Tables

aphelion	The point on an orbit that is farthest from the Sun.
apogee	The point on its orbit at which the Moon is farthest from the Earth.
appulse	The apparently close approach of two celestial objects; two planets, or a planet and star.
astronomical unit	(AU) The mean distance of the Earth from the Sun, 149,597,870 km.
celestial equator	The great circle on the celestial sphere that is in the same plane as the Earth's equator.
celestial sphere	The apparent sphere surrounding the Earth on which all celestial bodies (stars, planets, etc.) seem to be located.
conjunction	The point in time when two celestial objects have the same celestial longitude. In the case of the Sun and a planet, superior conjunction occurs when the planet lies on the far side of the Sun (as seen from Earth). For Mercury and Venus, inferior conjuction occurs when they pass between the Sun and the Earth.
direct motion	Motion from west to east on the sky.
ecliptic	The apparent path of the Sun across the sky throughout the year. Also: the plane of the Earth's orbit in space.
elongation	The point at which an inferior planet has the greatest angular distance from the Sun, as seen from Earth.
equinox	The two points during the year when night and day have equal duration. Also: the points on the sky at which the ecliptic intersects the celestial equator. The vernal (spring) equinox is of particular importance in astronomy.
gibbous	The stage in the sequence of phases at which the illumination of a body lies between half and full. In the case of the Moon, the term is applied to phases between First Quarter and Full, and between Full and Last Quarter.
inferior planet	Either of the planets Mercury or Venus, which have orbits inside that of the Earth.
magnitude	The brightness of a star, planet or other celestial body. It is a logarithmic scale, where larger numbers indicate fainter brightness. A difference of 5 in magnitude indicates a difference of 100 in actual brightness, thus a first-magnitude star is 100 times as bright as one of sixth magnitude.
meridian	The great circle passing through the North and South Poles of a body and the observer's position; or the corresponding great circle on the celestial sphere that passes through the North and South Celestial Poles and also through the observer's zenith.
nadir	The point on the celestial sphere directly beneath the observer's feet, opposite the zenith.
occultation	The disappearance of one celestial body behind another, such as when stars or planets are hidden behind the Moon.
opposition	The point on a superior planet's orbit at which it is directly opposite the Sun in the sky.
perigee	The point on its orbit at which the Moon is closest to the Earth.
perihelion	The point on an orbit that is closest to the Sun.
retrograde motion	Motion from east to west on the sky.
superior planet	A planet that has an orbit outside that of the Earth.
vernal equinox	The point at which the Sun, in its apparent motion along the ecliptic, crosses the celestial equator from south to north. Also known as the First Point of Aries.
zenith	The point directly above the observer's head.
zodiac	A band, streching 8° on either side of the ecliptic, within which the Moon and planets appear to move. It consists of twelve equal areas, originally named after the constellation that once lay within it.

The Constellations

There are 88 constellations covering the whole of the celestial sphere, but 4 of these in the northern hemisphere (Camelopardalis, Cassiopeia, Cepheus and Ursa Minor) can never be seen (even in part) from a latitude of 35°S, so are omitted from this table. The names themselves are expressed in Latin, and the names of stars are frequently given by Greek letters (see next page) followed by the genitive of the constellation name. The genitives and English names of the various constellations are included

Name	Genitive	Abbr.	English name
Andromeda	Andromedae	And	Andromeda
Antlia	Antliae	Ant	Air Pump
Apus	Apodis	Aps	Bird of Paradise
Aquarius	Aquarii	Aqr	Water Bearer
Aquila	Aquilae	Aql	Eagle
Ara	Arae	Ara	Altar
Aries	Arietis	Ari	Ram
Auriga	Aurigae	Aur	Charioteer
Boötes	Boötis	Boo	Herdsman
Caelum	Caeli	Cae	Burin
Cancer	Cancri	Cnc	Crab
Canes Venatici	Canum Venaticorum	CVn	Hunting Dogs
Canis Major	Canis Majoris	CMa	Big Dog
Canis Minor	Canis Minoris	CMi	Little Dog
Capricornus	Capricorni	Cap	Sea Goat
Carina	Carinae	Car	Keel
Centaurus	Centauri	Cen	Centaur
Cetus	Ceti	Cet	Whale
Chamaeleon	Chamaeleontis	Cha	Chameleon
Circinus	Circini	Cir	Compasses
Columba	Columbae	Col	Dove
Coma Berenices	Comae Berenices	Com	Berenice's Hair
Corona Australis	Coronae Australis	CrA	Southern Crown
Corona Borealis	Coronae Borealis	CrB	Northern Crown
Corvus	Corvi	Crv	Crow
Crater	Crateris	Crt	Cup
Crux	Crucis	Cru	Southern Cross
Cygnus	Cygni	Cyg	Swan
Delphinus	Delphini	Del	Dolphin
Dorado	Doradus	Dor	Dorado
Draco	Draconis	Dra	Dragon
Equuleus	Equulei	Equ	Little Horse
Eridanus	Eridani	Eri	River Eridanus
Fornax	Fornacis	For	Furnace
Gemini	Geminorum	Gem	Twins
Grus	Gruis	Gru	Crane
Hercules	Herculis	Her	Hercules
Horologium	Horologii	Hor	Clock
Hydra	Hydrae	Hya	Water Snake
Hydrus	Hydri	Hyi	Lesser Water Snake
Indus	Indi	Ind	Indian
Lacerta	Lacertae	Lac	Lizard
Leo	Leonis	Leo	Lion
Leo Minor	Leonis Minoris	LMi	Little Lion
Lepus	Leporis	Lep	Hare
Libra	Librae	Lib	Scales
Lupus	Lupi	Lup	Wolf
Lynx	Lyncis	Lyn	Lynx
Lyra	Lyrae	Lyr	Lyre
Mensa	Mensae	Men	Table Mountain
Microscopium	Microscopii	Mic	Microscope
Monoceros	Monocerotis	Mon	Unicorn
Musca	Muscae	Mus	Fly
Norma	Normae	Nor	Set Square
Octans	Octantis	Oct	Octant
Ophiuchus	Ophiuchi	Oph	Serpent Bearer
Orion	Orionis	Ori	Orion
Pavo	Pavonis	Pav	Peacock
Pegasus	Pegasi	Peg	Pegasus
Perseus	Persei	Per	Perseus
Phoenix	Phoenicis	Phe	Phoenix
Pictor	Pictoris	Pic	Painter's Easel
Pisces	Piscium	Psc	Fishes
Piscis Austrinus	Piscis Austrini	PsA	Southern Fish
Puppis	Puppis	Pup	Stern
Pyxis	Pyxidis	Pyx	Compass
Reticulum	Reticuli	Ret	Net
Sagitta	Sagittae	Sge	Arrow
Sagittarius	Sagittarii	Sgr	Archer
Scorpius	Scorpii	Sco	Scorpion
Sculptor	Sulptoris	Scu	Sculptor
Scutum	Scuti	Sct	Shield
Serpens	Serpentis	Ser	Serpent
Sextans	Sextantis	Sex	Sextant
Taurus	Tauri	Tau	Bull
Telescopium	Telescopii	Tel	Telescope
Triangulum	Trianguli	Tri	Triangle
Triangulum Australe	Trianguli Australis	TrA	Southern Triangle
Tucana	Tucanae	Tuc	Toucan
Ursa Major	Ursae Majoris	UMa	Great Bear
Vela	Velorum	Vel	Sails
Virgo	Virginis	Vir	Virgin
Volans	Volantis	Vol	Flying Fish
Vulpecula	Vulpeculae	Vul	Fox

The Greek Alphabet

α	Alpha	ε	Epsilon	ι	Iota	ν	Nu	ρ	Rho	φ (φ) Phi
β	Beta	ζ	Zeta	κ	Kappa	ξ	Xi	σ (ς)	Sigma	χ Chi
γ	Gamma	η	Eta	λ	Lambda	o	Omicron	τ	Tau	ψ Psi
δ	Delta	θ (ϑ)	Theta	μ	Mu	π	Pi	υ	Upsilon	ω Omega

Some common asterisms

Belt of Orion	δ, ε and ζ Orionis
Cat's Eyes	λ and υ Scorpii
Circlet	γ, θ, ι, λ and κ Piscium
False Cross	ε and ι Carinae and δ and κ Velorum
Fish Hook	α, β, δ and π Scorpii
Head of Cetus	α, γ, ξ², μ and λ Ceti
Head of Hydra	δ, ε, ζ, η, ρ and σ Hydrae
Job's Coffin	α, β, γ and δ Delphini
Keystone	ε, ζ, η and π Herculis
Kids	ε, ζ and η Aurigae
Milk Dipper	ζ, γ, σ, φ and λ Sagittarii
Pot	= Saucepan
Saucepan	ι, θ, ζ, ε, δ and η Orionis
Sickle	α, η, γ, ζ, μ and ε Leonis
Southern Pointers	α and β Centauri
Square of Pegasus	α, β and γ Pegasi with α Andromedae
Sword of Orion	θ and ι Orionis
Teapot	γ, ε, δ, λ, φ, σ, τ and ζ Sagittarii
Water Jar	γ, η, κ and ζ Aquarii
Y of Aquarius	= Water Jar

Acknowledgements

Sjbmgrtl, p.12 (Comet McNaught) [https://commons.wikimedia.org/wiki/File.Sat_comet_WEB.jpg]

Basilicofresco, p.12 (Murchison Meteorite) [https://commons.wikimedia.org/wiki/File:Murchison_crop.jpg]

Damian Peach, Hamble, Hants; p.13 (Comet Lovejoy)

peresanz/Shutterstock; p.21 (Orion)

Arthur Page, p.27 (False Cross); p.33 (Crux & Coalsack); p.59 (Milky Way); p.63 (Grus); p.69 (Corona Australis)

European Southern Observatory, p.51 (Omega Centauri) [https://www.eso.org/public/images/eso1119b/]

European Southen Observatory, p.75 (SMC & 47 Tucanae) [https://www.eso.org/public/images/eso1714a/]

European Southern Observatory, p.87 (LMC over Paranal)
[https://www.eso.org/public/images/2016-04-04-paranal-magellan-cc/]

Steve Edberg, La Cañada, California: all other constellation photographs

Further Information

Books

Bone, Neil (1993), *Observer's Handbook: Meteors*, George Philip, London & Sky Publ. Corp., Cambridge, Mass.

Cook, J., ed. (1999), *The Hatfield Photographic Lunar Atlas*, Springer-Verlag, New York

Dunlop, Storm (1999), *Wild Guide to the Night Sky*, HarperCollins, London

Dunlop, Storm (2012), *Practical Astronomy*, 3rd edn, Philip's, London

Dunlop, Storm, Rükl, Antonin & Tirion, Wil (2005), *Collins Atlas of the Night Sky*, HarperCollins, London

Ellyard, David & Tirion, Wil (2008) *Southern Sky Guide*, 3rd edition, Cambridge University Press, Cambridge

Heifetz, Milton & Tirion, Wil (2012), *A Walk through the Southern Sky: A Guide to Stars, Consellations and Their Legends*, 3rd edn, Cambridge University Press, Cambridge

O'Meara, Stephen J. (2008), *Observing the Night Sky with Binoculars*, Cambridge University Press, Cambridge

Ridpath, Ian, ed. (2004), *Norton's Star Atlas*, 20th edn, Pi Press, New York

Ridpath, Ian, ed. (2003), *Oxford Dictionary of Astronomy*, 2nd edn, Oxford University Press, Oxford

Ridpath, Ian & Tirion, Wil (2004), *Collins Gem - Stars*, HarperCollins, London

Ridpath, Ian & Tirion, Wil (2011), *Collins Pocket Guide Stars and Planets*, 4th edn, HarperCollins, London

Ridpath, Ian & Tirion, Wil (2012), *Monthly Sky Guide*, 9th edn, Cambridge University Press

Rükl, Antonín (1990), *Hamlyn Atlas of the Moon*, Hamlyn, London & Astro Media Inc., Milwaukee

Rükl, Antonín (2004), *Atlas of the Moon*, Sky Publishing Corp., Cambridge, Mass.

Scagell, Robin (2000), *Philip's Stargazing with a Telescope*, George Philip, London

Sky & Telescope (2017), *Astronomy 2018*, Australian Sky & Telescope, Quasar Publishing, Georges Hall, NSW

Tirion, Wil (2011), *Cambridge Star Atlas*, 4th edn, Cambridge University Press, Cambridge

Tirion, Wil & Sinnott, Roger (1999), *Sky Atlas 2000.0*, 2nd edn, Sky Publishing Corp., Cambridge, Mass. & Cambridge University Press, Cambridge

Journals

Astronomy, Astro Media Corp., 21027 Crossroads Circle, P.O. Box 1612, Waukesha, WI 53187-1612 USA. http://www.astronomy.com

Astronomy Now, Pole Star Publications, PO Box 175, Tonbridge, Kent TN10 4QX UK. http://www.astronomynow.com

Sky at Night Magazine, BBC publications, London. http://skyatnightmagazine.com

Sky & Telescope, Sky Publishing Corp., Cambridge, MA 02138-1200 USA. http://www.skyandtelescope.com/

Societies

British Astronomical Association, Burlington House, Piccadilly, London W1J 0DU.
http://www.britastro.org/

The principal British organization for amateur astronomers (with some professional members), particularly for those interested in carrying out observational programmes. Its membership is, however, worldwide. It publishes fully refereed, scientific papers and other material in its well-regarded journal.

Federation of Astronomical Societies, Secretary: Ken Sheldon, Whitehaven, Maytree Road, Lower Moor, Pershore, Worcs. WR10 2NY. http://www.fedastro.org.uk/fas/

An organization that is able to provide contact information for local astronomical societies in the United Kingdom.

Royal Astronomical Society, Burlington House, Piccadilly, London W1J 0BQ. http://www.ras.org.uk/
The premier astronomical society, with membership primarily drawn from professionals and experienced amateurs. It has an exceptional library and is a designated centre for the retention of certain classes of astronomical data. Its publications are the standard medium for dissemination of astronomical research.

Society for Popular Astronomy, 36 Fairway, Keyworth, Nottingham NG12 5DU.
http://www.popastro.com/
A society for astronomical beginners of all ages, which concentrates on increasing members' understanding and enjoyment, but which does have some observational programmes. Its journal is entitled *Popular Astronomy*.

Software

Planetary, Stellar and Lunar Visibility, (Planetary and eclipse freeware): Alcyone Software, Germany.
http://www.alcyone.de
Redshift, Redshift-Live. http://www.redshift-live.com/en/
Starry Night & Starry Night Pro, Sienna Software Inc., Toronto, Canada. http://www.starrynight.com

Internet sources

There are numerous sites with information about all aspects of astronomy, and all of those have numerous links. Although many amateur sites are excellent, treat any statements and data with caution. The sites listed below offer accurate information. Please note that the URLs may change. If so, use a good search engine, such as Google, to locate the information source.

Information

Astronomical data (inc. eclipses) HM Nautical Almanac Office: http://astro.ukho.gov.uk
Auroral information Michigan Tech: http://www.geo.mtu.edu/weather/aurora/
Comets JPL Solar System Dynamics: http://ssd.jpl.nasa.gov/
American Meteor Society: http://amsmeteors.org/
Deep-sky objects Saguaro Astronomy Club Database: http://www.virtualcolony.com/sac/
Eclipses: NASA Eclipse Page: http://eclipse.gsfc.nasa.gov/eclipse.html
Ice in Space (Southern Hemisphere Online Astronomy Forum) http://www.iceinspace.com.au/index.php?home
Moon (inc. Atlas) Inconstant Moon: http://www.inconstantmoon.com/
Planets Planetary Fact Sheets: http://nssdc.gsfc.nasa.gov/planetary/planetfact.html
Satellites (inc. International Space Station)
Heavens Above: http://www.heavens-above.com/
Visual Satellite Observer: http://www.satobs.org/
Star Chart http://www.skyandtelescope.com/observing/interactive-sky-watching-tools/interactive-sky-chart/
What's Visible
Skyhound: http://www.skyhound.com/sh/skyhound.html
Skyview Cafe: http://www.skyviewcafe.com

Institutes and Organizations

European Space Agency: http://www.esa.int/
International Dark-Sky Association: http://www.darksky.org/
Jet Propulsion Laboratory: http://www.jpl.nasa.gov/
Lunar and Planetary Institute: http://www.lpi.usra.edu/
National Aeronautics and Space Administration: http://www.hq.nasa.gov/
Solar Data Analysis Center: http://umbra.gsfc.nasa.gov/
Space Telescope Science Institute: http://www.stsci.edu/